IN PLACE OF WAR

In Place of War

An Inquiry into

Nonviolent National Defense

Prepared by a working party of

The American Friends

Service Committee

Grossman Publishers • New York, 1967

Library of Congress Catalog Card Number: 67-21234

Manufactured in the United States of America.
Second Printing

IN PLACE OF WAR

Foreword

Throughout the fifty years since its inception the American Friends Service Committee has held to its Quaker testimony against war. This testimony grows out of faith in God and belief in the sacredness of human personality.

During recent years, as occasion has warranted, working parties have been appointed to prepare reports for the American Friends Service Committee, dealing with issues of war and peace. These reports have included *The United States and the Soviet Union*, in 1949, *Steps to Peace*, in 1952, *Speak Truth to Power*, in 1955, *A New China Policy*, in 1965, and *Peace in Vietnam*, in 1966.

In 1965 a working party was appointed by the Peace Education Division of the AFSC to prepare a report on the Nonviolent Defense of a Nation. If the United States were to disarm as a matter of considered policy, could measures and policies based on nonviolence provide effective means of national defense?

This question in the contemporary context of poised missiles, of guerilla and counter-guerilla war, of burning villages and revolutionary struggle, suggests a turn of events which, on the face of it, seems quite remote. Nations do not seem to be close to beating their swords into plowshares, or their missiles into tractors. Even so, to think about such change is scarcely irrelevant to many of the problems which now confront the world, including the problem of withdrawal from irrational and unworkable military commitments, the problem of bringing an end to cold war, the problem of raising the level of life of the world's people by the constructive use of our minds and materials, and the problem of building a stable international community.

With the confidence born of a sense of great need for "a revolution in feeling, in sensitivity, in orientation, in the spirit of man," as A. J. Muste once wrote, this working party has completed its task, believing that it has been exploring uncharted areas which, eventually, pioneer nations must actually occupy and there establish a new world of nonviolence if the human family is to survive.

Members of the working party on IN PLACE OF WAR
Peace Education Division, American Friends Service
Committee, 1965-1966.

James E. Bristol, Secretary
Stephen G. Cary
William Davidon
George Lakey
Sidney Lens
Stewart Meacham
A. J. Muste
Mulford Q. Sibley
John M. Swomley, Jr.
Charles Walker

Mark Morris, staff writer

Contents

Introduction

In these times of vast and terrible wars—a century which has seen genocide introduced and given a place of utility if not of honor in the strategic armories of the great powers—talk about peace-making seems wistful, and peace itself seems at best a distant dream. The United Nations, for all its hope and promise, is not yet in a position to mediate and arbitrate, or to contain within a context of law, the disputes which arise involving the great powers. Disarmament is far from accomplished. Cultural exchange is a contribution to peace, but two world wars in this century are proof that more than that is needed if peace is to be assured. Moral idealism and a sense of the essential unity of mankind are necessary if there is to be peace in the world, but these very resources can be appropriated and put to the service of powerful war machines once the techniques of mass indoctrination are brought into play. And even if the one perfect plan for economic justice and social change were known, the world in the nuclear age does not dare wait until the war-causing problems have all been solved before dealing directly with the fact of war. Doubtless if world government, disarmament, cultural exchange, moral idealism, and broad programs of social justice all were combined with sufficient authority and effectiveness to remove the threat of nuclear war, there would be no need to ask whether these may not be alternative means which nations may employ to take the place of war when disputes arise. But since this condition does not now exist, it is desperately necessary that nations adopt other forms of national defense than war with military weapons. Otherwise, in the name of liberation and national security, governments resorting to the use of modern weapons will be increasingly drawn into contests of power which will destroy the very societies and civilizations they are trying to defend.

This book is the product of a small working party asked by the Program on Nonviolence of the American Friends Service Committee's Peace Education Division to prepare a report on the nonviolent defense of a nation. The working party realizes that its report is far from being a final answer to the questions with which it attempts to deal. At best the report may stimulate wider consideration of a controversial and highly speculative subject which is of importance not only to pacifists but to military-minded people as well, for the study of nonviolent civilian defense may indeed provide the key to the survival of civilization.

DEFINITIONS

The term *nonviolence* refers to (1) abstention from violence on the basis of a moral or religious principle or belief system or (2) the behavior of people abstaining from the use of violence in a conflict situation.

Nonviolent action refers to methods of protest, resistance, and intervention without physical violence in which members of the nonviolent group do or refuse to do certain things. Participants in nonviolent action may or may not be adherents to nonviolence in principle.[1]

The concept of nonviolent defense or civilian defense involves the extension of nonviolent action into a practical substitute for military defense and nuclear deterrence. It may also be viewed as an outgrowth of the post-Dulles United States defense orientation of proportionate response—that is, the strategy that best achieves stated aims of foreign policy. The process of changing over to nonviolent defense is termed *transarmament*.[2]

In this study we use interchangeably the terms *nonviolent defense* and *civilian defense*. The latter term has been employed by scholars in several countries, primarily England, who are working on many of the concepts and problems we deal with in this study.[3]

A PEACE EDUCATION SERVICE

In publishing this working party study as an educational service, the Peace Education Division of the American Friends Service Committee hopes that a wider consideration of civilian defense may encourage and lead to new and revolutionary techniques and strategies for dealing with international conflict.

This study will be a disappointment to those readers who expect a neat blueprint of irresistible nonviolent power applied to international conflict, for such a blueprint is not here. Those

---

[1] These definitions are based on the work of Gene Sharp and Adam Roberts, ed., *Civilian Defense* (London: Peace News, 1964).

[2] The term *transarmament* was originated by Theodor Ebert.

[3] See bibliography. There are two reasons for our decision not to use the term *civilian defense* exclusively. In this country it is often confused with the very different concept of *civil defense*. The term *nonviolent defense* is descriptive of the basic approach; *civilian defense* specifies the nonmilitary context of the effort. The terms are mutually supplementary.

who read expecting to be challenged by a ringing moral appeal to all men of good will to lay aside their arms, come what may, will also be disappointed for such an appeal is not here.

Instead, this study attempts to assess the practical possibilities of maintaining independence and national integrity without arms in the face of hostile aggression. Moral idealism would play an essential role, but the working party has accepted the burden of attempting to prove its case in terms of the practical results which can be reasonably anticipated rather than in terms of the validity of the ideals which may motivate the effort.

The working party has not proved its case in the sense that its conclusions are beyond dispute. Even so, if some are encouraged by this paper to lend their minds and hearts to the consideration of the defense of the nation without resort to modern weapons of war, but relying instead on non-military resources for resistance to tyranny and aggression, the efforts of the working party will have been useful.

From time to time the American Friends Service Committee has been responsible for working party papers on issues of pressing public concern, and it has sponsored or published such papers with varying expressions of endorsement and support. These papers have included:

The United States and The Soviet Union, Yale University, New Haven, 1949.

Steps to Peace, A.F.S.C., Philadelphia, 1952.

Speak Truth to Power, A.F.S.C., Philadelphia, 1955.

A New China Policy, Yale University, New Haven, 1965.

Peace in Vietnam, Hill & Wang, New York, 1966.

The Peace Education Division commends this paper to those thoughtful people, laymen and experts alike, who are troubled by the fact of modern war and the place it holds in the foreign policy of the nation. The Division hopes that discussion and thought about the issues raised here may enhance confidence among the people that national defense can be more prudently entrusted to the civilians themselves than to a lethally armed military establishment.

A Scenario

A NOTE TO THE READER

Here we use a technique which has come to be known as the "scenario." Readers of the nuclear strategist Herman Kahn are familiar with this technique. It represents, simply, the thinking through in narrative form of one possible course of events in order to stimulate the imagination and make it easier to tease out the implications hidden in a given sequence of events.

The scenario, then, is not a prediction of what *will* happen. We leave prophecy to the prophets. We hope earnestly that our rather grim scenario will never take place, but the implications of reliance on nuclear weapons for national security must nevertheless be faced. We believe this narrative exercise helps toward that end, and leads us to the point where alternative means of national defense can seriously be considered. It does this by presenting a situation in which the Government of the United States decides to build the entire defense of the country on the concept of nonviolent national defense.

The City of Denver was destroyed by a nuclear bomb just ten years after the Chinese exploded their first nuclear device in 1964. That first Chinese nuclear test had been viewed soberly by most nuclear weapons strategists at the time. As Secretary of Defense McNamara put it, "The danger to the other nations of the world increases geometrically with the increase in the number of nations possessing those warheads." At the same time reassurances had been expressed, based on the belief that a decade would pass before China or any other new nuclear power could accumulate a nuclear stockpile, and an even longer period would be needed to develop reliable delivery systems.

These reassurances failed to reckon with nuclear weapons proliferation. After the United States began to supply them to her allies, merchants in illicit arms traffic managed to acquire them, and they eventually were bought by even the smaller and poorer countries as status symbols. Within a few years nuclear bombs had become both cheap and accessible. China sold them, cash on the barrelhead, to small nations whose friendship she courted. Fortunately, missile delivery system technology did not advance as rapidly as the spread of bombs themselves; but everyone assumed that this too would come in time.

For a few years after China's first bomb test the United States had continued to adhere to its basic strategy of nuclear deterrence. As developed by the United States, nuclear deterrence depended on the calculated capacity of United States armed forces to survive attack with enough strength left to be able to do more damage to an aggressor than the attack would be worth. This required: (1) the ability to identify the aggressor, (2) the ability to survive the aggression, (3) the ability to hit the aggressor with surviving weapons, (4) the ability to retain, after the exchange with the aggressor, deterrent capacity with respect to other possible aggressors, and (5) the ability after survival to rebuild.

The deterrence system worked in the sense that there was no

*nuclear attack in the twenty-nine years between Nagasaki and
Denver (assuming that the Denver explosion was not an accident). But in a larger sense problems in deterrence strategy
were never resolved. It remained clear that the United States
would survive a massive nuclear onslaught very poorly, if at all.
Although military leaders urged the development of an anti-
missile missile system, this was not done. A major reason was
that the American public would not accept the massive underground shelter program that anti-missile missiles would necessitate. Many feared that a realistic program would involve
moving the entire civilization underground.*

*Others claimed that since insects can withstand ten times
as much radiation as birds, the people would emerge from
their shelters after a nuclear holocaust to find the ecological
balance upset, their world taken over by insects. Perhaps some
of the insects would be monstrous due to genetic change
caused by radiation. To meet this problem a high Pentagon
official proposed that we "stockpile" birds. This was not done.
Few realistic preparations were made to enable the country
to withstand nuclear attack.*

*The only adequately equipped shelters were those for gov-
ernment officials, the military, and, in a few private shelters
the managers of large corporations. The ability to survive
nuclear attack was always gravely in doubt, though few of
the American people understood this.*

*However, nuclear war did not occur. The proliferation of
nuclear weapons did not at first complicate the situation. There
was little or no danger of an attack on the United States from
Canada or Mexico, even though each acquired nuclear weapons. Except for the Soviet Union, no country possessing the
bomb had reliable means of accurate missile delivery to
United States targets. From the time of the Cuba crisis of
1962 onward there had been a working acknowledgment between the United States and the Soviet Union that each had
achieved the deterrent situation with respect to the other.
Each knew that the other could hit so hard that even after an*

all-out first strike life would surely disintegrate for the side receiving the second blow as well as the first. Each conveyed to the other its acknowledgment of this basic situation in a variety of ways. Statesmen and military experts tended to agree that deterrence had at last become absolute; they believed that the bomb on both sides cancelled itself out. Following the Chinese bomb tests of 1964 and 1965 these reassuring predictions were rudely upset by the spread of nuclear weapons among the erstwhile non-nuclear powers.

The spread meant that eventually the situation could not be managed or controlled once missile delivery systems also had spread. To delay the spread of delivery systems the United States and the Soviet Union cooperated to keep China from becoming a missile-launching nation. Both stepped up their espionage and their electronic surveillance of China, and of other suspect countries, and exchanged information. Each in its own way stated separately that the acquisition and testing of ICBM's by any nation not then possessing them would be considered a hostile act.

To the satisfaction of each, China apparently bowed to the inevitable and did not move on from nuclear weapons development to ICBM development. After a time the stability of the nuclear deterrence stalemate returned to international life, mildly agitated by the highly remote chance of an accidental war or of an anti-missile-missile breakthrough. Actually, if an accident had occurred, it would not have been likely to start a war. Safeguards were available which would allow time and communication to determine that it was indeed an accident rather than an attack.

This relatively benign state of affairs in nuclear policy was, from the point of view of the United States, in sharp contrast to deepening frustration in foreign policy. France, a prime beneficiary of Marshall Plan aid after World War II, became first prosperous and then a rival. She succeeded in denying the United States the military and economic voice the United States felt it deserved in Europe. The Labor government which came into power in England in 1964 put frustration of the Washington-endorsed multilateral nuclear force high on its agenda.

In 1970, the world's first constitutionally elected Communist government came to power in Italy. Western politicians made dire predictions but these were soon proved mistaken. As it turned out, the new Italian government supported more strongly than its predecessor the alliance of the United States-Europe-Soviet Union against China, the Southeast Asian nations, and most of Africa. This opened the way the following year for the reunification of Germany. The new coalition government proved less intractable than the old West German government. Most American officials were pleased with these developments.

While Europe, except for France, was comparatively tranquil, other parts of the globe were not. After years of bloodshed, the fighting finally died out in Southeast Asia. Officially the area had been "demilitarized" by the United Nations, but Chinese influence remained strong and was growing in Africa as well. The embittered South African regime had grown more inflexible and a bloodbath in that unhappy country appeared inevitable. South America had seen a decade of increasingly bitter guerrilla warfare. At the time of the Denver explosion, 100,000 United States military advisers were on that continent, most of them in Brazil. An uprising was predicted momentarily in Chile.

The United Nations had not grown much in influence but it had survived. China had been admitted years before. At that time Formosa withdrew from the international body. The United States engaged in extensive trade with China but still had not established diplomatic relations, though the Chinese Mission to the United Nations maintained a large embassy in New York.

Though the sincerity of the humanitarian aims of American foreign policy was widely acknowledged, the billions of dollars invested in economic and social development of new nations had less impact than the vastly greater American military aid. The United States rarely escaped alliance with reactionary elements in those countries where military aid was large. Massive aid programs were carried out but they raised the standard of living of the poor only slightly, and they did not prevent the rapid growth of discontent. This, coupled with expanding Chinese influence, meant that the United States continuously feared the outbreak of small wars on many fronts. Thus much of the social progress that could have been made was not realized.

The sluggish American economy, though stimulated by defense contracts, economic aid, and the continuing nuclear arms race, to say nothing of costly though dramatic adventures in space, experienced a rising rate of unemployment. Domestic problems piled up. Though a guaranteed national income had been established two years earlier, there was no over-all plan to offset the effects of automation. A series of civil rights acts failed to quell rising Negro discontent. Brave efforts to contain urban blight failed to halt the rising crime rate.

Years of unavailing protest against American military intervention had demoralized left-wing elements in the United States. They had gained their greatest strength in the fight against unemployment. This movement died with the Guaranteed National Income Act of 1972, which assured each adult American citizen a monthly income administered through Social Security. Though this measure was inadequate, it caused the collapse of most groups in the left-wing coalition, other than a handful devoted to nonviolent direct action, which continued apparently hopeless protests against militarism and the regimentation of society.

The American public, besieged by the advertisers of consumer goods, grew increasingly apathetic. An erratic right-wing political movement mushroomed, inconsistently appealing to isolationist attitudes and at the same time calling for interventionist actions advocating both "less government" and increased power for the FBI.

Thus the decade following the first Chinese bomb test was marked by disintegration of the United States-Soviet monopoly on nuclear weapons and deepening political and economic crisis for American policy. This was the situation in 1974 when two events occurred which changed history: (1) The United States caught two men smuggling a Chinese-made thermonuclear bomb ashore a few miles north of Gold Beach on the Oregon coast; (2) Two weeks later the city of Denver was completely destroyed by a thermonuclear explosion.

No connection between these two events was ever established. The two smugglers said that they had been hired by two strangers to meet a launch and load a large crate from it onto a rented truck equipped with a loading derrick. They had been caught near this spot. They said they were to deliver the truck with the crate, the contents of which had not been revealed to them, to the two strangers at a spot thirty miles north of San Francisco.

After the arrest of the smugglers the two strangers did not show up at the rendezvous and nothing more was ever learned regarding the incident. No connection was ever established linking the arrested men with prior illegal activity of any sort. The Chinese bomb bore a number which could have been a serial number. It was 279. It was in the ten megaton class and was triggered with a device which could be activated by a short wave signal.

News of this incident was at first tightly suppressed. It was not made public until after the destruction of Denver.

The Denver obliteration occurred at 3:42 A.M. on a clear night two weeks later. Ground Zero appeared to have been at a point near the southwestern border of the Rocky Mountain Arsenal which lay to the northeast of the city proper. There was some doubt as to whether the bomb explosion had been inside or outside the arsenal area. There was never any question as to the fact that the bomb had been in the multimegaton class, but there were disputes as to its exact rating, estimates running from ten megatons all the way up to twenty-

five. One expert speculated that it may have been an airdrop. This was generally discounted although a SAC bomber, on routine patrol, armed with a nuclear weapon, had been overhead at the moment of the explosion. No trace of it was ever found.

Within fifteen minutes after the explosion, the President's cabinet and staff had begun to assemble at the White House Emergency Control Center. Everyone was stunned. The news from Denver was unclear. Total casualties were estimated at about one-half million. The city was completely pulverized, flattened, burned out. Fallout danger to surrounding areas had not yet been calculated. Mounting panic was reported across the nation.

In the Emergency Control Center two members of the Joint Chiefs of Staff argued that an immediate all-out attack on China was called for. "This is the chance we've been waiting for!" said one. Others urged caution. Tempers flared as they awaited the President's arrival.

Meanwhile predetermined emergency precautions were initiated. To quiet nationwide unrest, a prerecorded television message from the President was released. It assured the nation that the situation was under control and urged people to stay home and keep listening to radio and television. The tape, prepared for use in any sort of emergency, was played repeatedly, interspersed with vague but carefully worded reports on the Denver "accident." People were instructed to remain in sheltered areas until fallout danger was determined.

The Secretary of State in the control center initiated calls via "hot-line" to all major powers, friend and enemy, assuring on the authority of the President that no drastic steps would be taken without notice.

On his way to the control center, the President stopped at his White House family quarters. His wife was in tears. He hugged her. "I'll be calm in a minute," she said. "You go ahead and we will be along shortly."

His daughter was gazing out a window. He asked what she

was doing. "I'm trying to decide," she said cryptically, and picked up a guitar and put it in its case.

He started to speak, but knew there wasn't time. He hurried away.

The President opened the meeting with the proposal that the cities of the United States be evacuated and searched. This was opposed because it would cause panic and would be impossible to evacuate every city in the whole country. The Attorney General gave assurances that FBI searches were underway in all major cities. The CIA had all its men working double shifts. The Secretary of State pointed out that if bomb smuggling were actually the problem, it would be better to be without shelters so that precipitous and misconceived retaliatory action would not be a compelling temptation.

By this time the group advocating immediate all-out attack on China had picked up supporters and urged prompt action. An opposing faction urged destruction of two Chinese cities the size of Denver. This developed into a dispute over whether a warning should be given. There was also argument as to the probable Russian response and the likelihood of escalation.

"This is no time to hesitate!" a general declared. "Our very existence is at stake! Are we going to sit here while China picks off city after city? How many Denvers do you need? Say the word and in twenty minutes China will be ashes."

"What would that accomplish?" asked the Attorney General. "If we were merely looking for an excuse to destroy China, I'm sure the CIA could manufacture a better one. Let me remind you that we don't know that the Denver explosion was caused by a Chinese bomb. Might it not have been an accident? Might not some other nation have caused it?"

"It's clear now that we made a mistake," said a presidential assistant, "when we didn't announce the capture of the Chinese bomb at Gold Beach. It'll be necessary to build a case pinning Denver on China before hitting her cities."

Another adviser broke in, "How do we know China did it? If the Denver explosion were caused by China, wouldn't it be coupled with a Chinese demand of some kind? Wouldn't the Chinese be saying, if you don't do such-and-such you lose another city?"

"Can't we safely assume that China had nothing to do with it?" asked the Secretary of Defense. "It makes no sense for a big power to explode a bomb on a single major city. They can't make us knuckle under that way. We can still wipe every weapon, every city, and every man, woman, and child in China right off the face of the earth and we probably would do it if we could pin Denver on Peking. Why should they run such a risk? They may be Communists but they aren't stupid."

"Who is being stupid?" asked the Secretary of State sharply. "Let us suppose China has two hundred bombs but no rocket delivery system. Intelligence indicates that this is the case. What good are those bombs stockpiled in China? None. Where would they be useful? Planted in hidden locations in or near strategic targets in the United States. If they could smuggle in and hide their bombs, they would solve their delivery problems at a tiny fraction of the cost of ICBM's. And they would achieve absolute accuracy, which is more than even we can say for our delivery systems."

"But they couldn't have smuggled that many bombs into the United States," objected the Director of the CIA, "we'd have caught them. Our security network is tops, you know that. We caught the men at Gold Beach practically before they had the bomb ashore."

"How can we be sure?" asked the Secretary of State. "After all, the men at Gold Beach were caught because of an anonymous phone call to the FBI. Maybe the Chinese were responsible for the smuggling operation—and maybe they wanted it to get caught."

"You mean the FBI was tipped off by the Chinese?" exploded the Secretary of Health, Education, and Welfare. "Why would they do that?"

"So we would be warned that they have us mined. The Russians have us deterred only because we know they can hit us. We have the Russians deterred for the same reason. Now the

Chinese want in on deterrence. We know that. Maybe this is their way of letting us know they have us. What could be better than getting us mined, then arranging a convenient interception of smugglers, and then underscoring the threat with the actual destruction of one of our cities?"

"Do you think that is what they have done?" asked the President.

"Frankly, I doubt it," replied the Secretary of Defense. "I think it is more likely that the captured bomb at Gold Beach is the first, not the two hundred and first they have slipped ashore. By arranging to get caught they pin us down with a single bomb precisely because we do not know for certain that it is the only one. As long as there is a serious possibility that two hunderd of our cities, or one hundred, or fifty are mined, we have had it. We just don't dare take the chance. If my guess is right—and it is sheer guess—then the destruction of Denver is, from their point of view, an unexpected bonus. It cinches the greatest bargain-basement military deterrence package in all of the history of war."

A silence fell. The President turned to the Secretary of Defense. "What is your analysis? What should we do?"

The Secretary began slowly. "If national security depended upon the possession of widest flexibility of nuclear weapon responses, if it depended upon the most rapid and accurate delivery systems, if it depended upon the largest nuclear arsenal, if it depended upon the number of weapons buried in impregnable silos or poised in the launching cradles of submarines cruising beneath the surface of the seas, if it depended upon our ability to take a recognizable photograph of any person on earth standing on a clear day in front of his dwelling and gazing into the sky, if it depended upon any or all of these capacities we would be a secure nation. Unfortunately, the day when national security depended upon such capacities is gone. Now we are faced with a situation to which neither our strength nor our weapons apply."

Several men protested. The President rapped for order.

The Defense Secretary continued. "You have asked what we should do. Our first task is to satisfy ourselves that the Denver explosion was not accidental, that the bomb was not our bomb. As all of you know, our fail-safe procedures are fool-proof. Despite the missing SAC bomber, I think we can discount the possibility that the bomb was American. Preliminary reports on trace elements in the fallout confirm this hypothesis."

"Except for one chance in a thousand," challenged an adviser.

"We have calculated that chance as less than one in three million," replied the Secretary.

"That's still a chance," said the adviser.

"Agreed," said the Secretary with a cold smile. "In this life nothing is certain but death and taxes, we are told. However, as a basis for action, we accept certain occurrences—or non-occurrences—to be of extremely high probability. I repeat, I am satisfied that the Denver bomb was not American in origin. Do we now have agreement on this point?"

After an uneasy silence the President murmured, "We do."

"The next task," continued the Secretary, "is to satisfy ourselves that the bomb was not delivered by missile. Here I think we can convince even college professors. All detection equipment was working perfectly up to the moment of explosion. There was not the slightest indication from any of the screening apparatus that an unidentified object had been approaching the Denver area at the time."

He paused and looked around. "This leaves us with the conclusion that the Denver explosion was caused by a smuggled bomb. The Attorney General has expressed doubt that China was the smuggler. What are the chances on this? Here we cannot be precise. The connection with the bomb seized at Gold Beach is, as they say, purely circumstantial.

"Exactly," said the Attorney General. "The smugglers may have been Indonesian or Cuban, Israeli or Arab—even French or British fascists precipitating a crisis which would put them in power."

"But what should we do? What action should we take?"
asked the President. "How can we see that no more American
cities are destroyed?"

A civilian adviser to the National Security Council who
had been silent spoke up. "We can announce secretly to the
Chinese that two of their cities will be destroyed in return for
Denver, and that if another American city is destroyed, we'll
take four Chinese cities."

There were expressions of approval.

"Ah, but suppose—" interrupted the Attorney General, "sup-
pose the Denver bomb was planted by some country other
than China. Your strategy would play right into their hands."

"Do you mean that we shouldn't retaliate at all?" asked the
President.

A general broke in. "And so we wipe away a tear and say,
'Goodbye, Denver.' And tomorrow, they—whoever they are—
pick off Forth Worth or Chicago."

"If there were something we could do to prevent this, I
would favor it," said the Attorney General. "So far that some-
thing has not been suggested. You say 'whoever they are.'
They could be anyone who has bought bombs from China.
We don't know as a fact that China had anything to do either
with the Denver bomb or the Gold Beach bomb."

There was a silence.

The President looked imploringly at all the men in the room.
"Surely there must be something we can do," he said. "We are
the most powerful nation in the history of the world. Tech-
nologically we are the most advanced. There must be some
reasonable course of action open to us."

"I can carry my analysis further," said the Defense Secretary.
"Among other factors, our present defense is based upon our
ability to identify the aggressor. In the present instance, this
condition does not prevail. Thus, in this situation it is impos-
sible to relate nuclear war preparations and capacity to na-
tional security. Gentlemen, I sincerely believe that tonight
marks the end of an era."

There were exclamations of surprise.

"Now you're getting weak-kneed," said a general. "After all, it's only one smuggled bomb. It's a bomb that by all rights the FBI should have intercepted."

The Attorney General countered, "Is it only a bomb or is it five hundred thousand people dead? And God knows how many more sicknesses and deaths from the fallout—or how many more bombs."

The President spoke. "We are the most powerful nation on earth and yet Denver is charred rubble. There are many forms of power. Our nuclear bomb power is no longer relevant. It no longer works."

"It's as though the United States were muscle-bound—like an aging athlete who is over-trained," said an adviser.

The Secretary of Defense spoke. "It's clear to me that the kind of power we need is the power to have stopped the Denver explosion before it happened. We thought we had it, with our prevention and retaliation capability factors—but it didn't work. In fact, it seems to me that these forms of defense may have encouraged the explosion. Our colossal military might has made other nations fear us. We have run up against the old story of civilian hatred every time we have had to send a few troops in to stabilize local government. Our high standard of living in contrast to other nations has made us envied. We perpetuated these conditions for reasons of defense—but now they serve instead as obstacles to the future security and well-being of the United States."

The Secretary of Commerce spoke up. "I agree. We kid ourselves that peace and military strength go hand in hand. In Vietnam what happened? We believed in the domino theory. We thought that if we pulled out we would lose not only Vietnam but the rest of Southeast Asia as well. It turned out that even our friends turned against us. And our enemies made hay."

"I'm no expert on nuclear weapons or foreign policy," the Secretary of Agriculture chimed in, "but in African and Latin

America the biggest single domestic problem is improvement of farming techniques and more efficient land utilization. American armed might is identified in the minds of people with propping up the few and keeping them in power against the wishes of the man, which spells further successes for Castroism and other brands of social revolution. We are caught backing the wrong horses in Latin America and in Africa, and nuclear weapons only distract us from real solutions."

"I think we are oversimplifying the problems we face," said the Secretary of State.

"But he does have a point," said the President.

The Defense Secretary spoke. "But where does the point carry us? What does it prove?"

"Do we think that just by being good we can get the world to treat us nice?" asked a senior five star general.

"Not at all," replied the Defense Secretary. "Our foreign policy has been based on the concept of proportionate response. Insurgency in Vietnam was not met with counter insurgency. We adopted the response to a particular situation that seemed most likely to achieve our policy goals. Let us not rule out the possibility that the answer today might lie in the creation of some sort of nonmilitary national defense."

In the continuing discussion it was agreed that the Defense Secretary would head a top level team to investigate alternative means of defense, including civilian direct action. For public consumption the Denver explosion was explained as an accident and attributed to the missing SAC bomber. The generals secured agreement that if intelligence should establish the identity of the country responsible for the bombing, retaliatory measures would be taken. The meeting lasted eleven hours.

In closing the meeting the President said, "It is impossible to know what our investigations of nonmilitary defense will reveal, but I am hopeful. I came to this meeting with the heaviest burden I have ever known, the burden of the destruction of Denver, the burden of a threatened nation. The burden *still weighs on me, but now there seems to be a chance that we can find and utilize new kinds of power equal to the demands of the thermonuclear age. I will pray that this is so."*

As they left the conference room, several men complimented the President on his closing remarks. Walking down the hallway they could hear his daughter's guitar. She was playing "We Shall Overcome."

"Now where the hell did she learn a song like that?" the President wondered.

(The scenario resumes on page 105)

1 | Nonviolence, War, and World Community

In an age of violence it may seem strange that nonviolent action is an acknowledged means of power. Nevertheless, the names of Gandhi and Martin Luther King symbolize power for social change in the very time of nuclear weapons and mass destruction. Both men have led movements of peaceful but militant social change against concentrations of armed power and their nonviolent followers have often prevailed.

The most pressing problem of our day is the problem of international conflict—of war, of violence between states committed to no common international framework of order. Can nonviolent action, which has the power to bring about change in the internal structure of an established social order, also be effective as a means of national defense? Far from being academic, theoretical, or abstractly moral, in the nuclear age this is a concrete, pressing, and practical question.

In the scenario we put together real elements of the actual situation we are in today and produced an imaginary story in which the United States began to consider a nonviolent system of national defense. Our purpose is to show that it would be logical and prudent to shift from military to nonviolent defense. It is an obligation of prudence, of morals, and of patriotism to consider the facts about the possibilities and to arrive at rational and considered judgments. We shall consider the dangers as well as the advantages of a nonviolent defense policy.

THE THREE USES OF NONVIOLENT ACTION

The conditions under which nonviolent struggle would be used in international conflict are different in kind from the conditions under which it has been used in domestic conflict. Unless these differences are understood and taken into account it is not possible to solve the problem of how, in international conflict, nonviolent initiatives can be taken, how decisions to use nonviolent sanctions can be made, and what nonviolent action may or may not be effective in particular situations.

In one sense the development of orderly processes for the resolution of international conflicts is in itself nonviolent. In this paper, however, we are focusing on the question of whether it is practical to resist armed forces nonviolently in international conflict instead of resisting with arms. The question assumes that any realistic policy must deal with the eventuality that in a given situation opportunities for mediation, negotiation, and peaceful settlement might be exhausted.[1]

Too often in the past the success of nonviolent action in

---

[1]In this study we have not dealt with the problems of peace-keeping through the United Nations. This resource in achieving a demilitarized world might be the subject of a later working party paper. Until it is dealt with, within the context of nonviolence, the task of coping with international conflict nonviolently will not have been complete. We are aware of the considerable amount of attention now being given this matter and we strongly support these efforts.

social protest movement has led to the assumption by peace-concerned people that it may be applied in the same way and with equal success to international conflict. This assumption has produced confusion and disappointment. For example, in the case of India's border disputes with Pakistan and China, India's use of armed force shocked many people, in spite of the fact that India had never claimed to be nonviolent in the defense of its borders and had not decided as a nation to rely upon nonviolent methods for national defense.

International conflict imposes its own conditions. If nonviolent defense is to be effective in international conflict, it is necessary that these conditions be understood and met. For purposes of clarification we identify three quite different purposes of nonviolent action. They differ according to the social context in which each is used.

1. *Nonviolent action as a means of social protest, social reform, and social revolution.*

The most dramatic use of nonviolent action has been as a means of social protest. Outstanding instances in this century have been the Indian independence struggle and the present civil rights movement in the United States.

Both of these movements achieved success against vastly superior forces, yet they were struggles of protest and reform rather than of total revolution. This was true even in India where, despite the avowed aim of independence from British rule, independence was so interpreted as to allow India a continuing place in the British Commonwealth of nations, a continuing reliance upon the British concepts and structures of justice and law, and continuing trade and commercial ties with British industrial and financial interests.

To launch and carry out this form of nonviolent struggle does not require corporate decision. Even a few can launch nonviolent protest and direct action against the existing system or authority of the state. Ultimate success will depend upon winning wide support, but the decision to initiate the struggle can be made by as few as two or three individuals.

A nonviolent movement can be organized in one of two ways. It might create a "parallel government" which eventually will take power, as in India, or it might press for reforms within the existing legal and social structure, as with the freedom movement in this country. Since the confrontation in both cases is with established authority, the impression is widespread that nonviolent action is essentially disruptive, that it can be used only to change or to overthrow, that it is even anti-state or anti-police. That is not so. Virtually always the goal of a nonviolent movement is to create a just and stable society, with the government, laws, and police that are entailed.

2. *Nonviolent action as a means of maintaining social order*

This use of nonviolent action is very different from its use in social protest.

Here nonviolent methods are used not to change the social order but to preserve it. That police have increasingly begun to use nonviolent methods is encouraging, for the police give (or should give) concrete expression to the conscience of the community through the enforcement of its laws. They acquire power over the members of society and at the same time the members of society acquire power over them. Police expression of community conscience is never completely satisfactory but, at its best, it is probably as good a way as any to express, day in and day out, the will of the community. This is especially true when police conduct is governed by an understanding of nonviolent methods.

So far these methods have been applied primarily to crowd control and riot prevention. Under circumstances in which police formerly had social permission to respond with violence —guns, clubs, fire hoses, or tear gas—specific nonviolent methods are being substituted with excellent results. As the quality of police training increases and improves, it is likely that there will be further application of nonviolent methods to police works; the current emphasis on the civil liberties of those under arrest exerts pressure in this direction.

However, an examination of the dynamics of nonviolence raises questions as to how far in the direction of nonviolence the police are likely to proceed. A practitioner of nonviolence aims to win over his opponent by refusing to respond with violence regardless of the provocation. This process becomes most powerful when the practitioner of nonviolence takes upon himself unmerited suffering. While it is possible to envision a society in which the police system is organized on this principle, the police of the United States today do not seem close to it.

In some respects British police have proceeded further in this direction than have American police. London bobbies normally do not carry guns. Yet instances of police brutality—and other problems—continue.

The limited nature of police experience in the practice of nonviolence may be particularly relevant to civilian defense, for in any large-scale application of nonviolent techniques the majority of the practitioners presumably would not be philosophically committed to nonviolence. Thus they could and would most readily participate in forms of nonviolent action which made limited demands upon them.

Nonviolent techniques are now widely used in the care of the mentally ill. During World War II conscientious objectors performing alternative service in mental hospitals expanded nonviolent concepts. In contrast to some forms of violent treatment of patients then acceptable, these men entirely renounced the use of violence and, in some cases, even the use of physical restraint. Patients responded positively and the number of violent incidents decreased. Though originated by men who were committed to nonviolence in principle, these nonviolent methods are now widely used by all concerned with the care of the mentally ill. Together with tranquilizing drugs introduced after the war, these methods have revolutionized the care of the mentally ill and have virtually eliminated overt violence from mental hospitals.

Nonviolent techniques are also being applied in prisons and jails. The use of grosser forms of physical violence is decreasing though the approach to the rehabilitation of those who have committed anti-social acts is still far from nonviolent. Obviously nonviolent reforms within institutions are not directly applicable to the use of nonviolent action in maintaining social order in society at large. Still, lessons might be learned.

A thornier problem is presented when those who are entrusted with law enforcement not only fail to perform their duty, but actually side with the lawless element. Who then enforces the law? Can private citizens then nonviolently uphold social order?

During the civil rights struggle in the United States this problem has been faced at times. Usually success depends upon getting the police to do their jobs rather than finding nonviolent resisters to try to do it for them. In a Pennsylvania town a Negro couple moved into a formerly all-white neighborhood and were in actual danger of their lives. The local police were lackadaisical and the state police were called away for duties elsewhere. A group committed to a discipline of nonviolence, including clergymen, gathered, hoping to be able to intervene if necessary between the mob and the family. The main problem was not how to find the courage to intervene but how to intervene with the demands of conscience and an expression of moral authority. How would they make themselves understood? How would they acquire access to the conflict as exponents of a view grounded in moral obligation? This was their problem. Fortunately in this case word got to the state police headquarters in time to cause a reversal of the plan to withdraw and the neighborhood was cleared without incident by the return of the state police.

It is our view that nonviolence is relevant to the maintenance of law and order as well as to social protest. The task is not to usurp the role of the police but to persuade them to fulfill their responsibilities as a means, and a very important one, whereby the community expresses its moral judgment. The police are at their best when using nonviolent methods.

This is an entirely different sort of exercise of nonviolent action from that of social protest. Nonviolence may be a creative force in both cases. But the relationships are different, the problems of access to the conflict are different, the methods are different, the temptations are different, and the rewards are different. Above all, the amount of carry-over from one type of action to the other has not been clearly established. The fact that an individual or a group has used nonviolent action effectively in social protest does not assure that the same individual or group will—or can—use nonviolent action with equal effectiveness in maintaining social order or community.

3. *Nonviolent action as a means of national defense*

How are serious conflicts to be dealt with when there is no law, or not enough law and acknowledged procedure to contain conflicts and keep them from becoming violent?

This question brings us to the nub of our study. Precisely this situation exists among the nations today. Although the vacuum is not total, it is sufficient to leave grave doubt that international conflict involving the use of nuclear weapons can be administratively forestalled by present world community resources.

What then can be done? Are nonviolent methods relevant to this kind of conflict? It is the purpose of this study to suggest an affirmative answer to this question.

First there must be clarity as to who can decide to use nonviolent action in defending a country. As we see it, the country itself must make this decision. It can only be made by those who are legitimately responsible for setting policy and for making decisions. In the United States this means the President, the Congress and Courts. The decision must be based on broad public understanding and support. At this point nonviolent national defense is quite different from social protest, where a few individuals can launch the action, consulting only their own consciences. It is not sufficient, where national defense is at stake and where conflict with an enemy is anticipated or underway, for any group, purely as a matter of conscience and operating on their own, to intervene with nonviolent resistance to deal with the enemy. Although sometimes suggested, this is quite unrealistic.

It is conceivable, of course, that in the event of war or threat of war, a nonviolent anti-war campaign could be mounted in protest against the military policies of the government, and could win such wide support that the government would either go out of power or else adopt a policy of nonmilitary defense. But this only reinforces our point. International conflict is conflict among nations—and only the nation can decide what sanctions and techniques will be used. Thus a national defense policy relying upon nonviolent means of struggle would be one in which the authority of the whole society and the government is committed to that policy should the country be invaded. With the moral influence and resources of the whole country behind the actions of the citizens, the conditions and situation would be very different than if citizens were acting alone.

Of this third level of nonviolent action, that of international conflict, much less is known than in the case of the other two. We will trace briefly the history of the use of nonviolent action in situations approximating national defense, suggest ways in which nonviolent defense might be organized, and consider the changes in foreign and domestic policy this would involve.

WAR, POLITICS, AND WORLD COMMUNITY

Carl von Clausewitz defined war as an "act of violence for the purpose of forcing the opponent to do one's will." Modern war with nuclear weapons has lost its link and its continuity with political purpose because the degree of violence which it entails has stripped diplomacy of the rationality on which international politics depends. Today politics must be extended and transformed into a substitute for war by other means, for new facts almost daily further confound the possibility of relating nuclear war to rational political purpose.

It is not our intention here to say again how dangerous and immoral war is, nor even to survey in detail the dangers of the present situation. We shall only offer a few sentences to remind us of the severe problems of defense which must be faced.

1. *China has the bomb.* No one knows how many she has or how long it will take her to accumulate an arsenal. But it is reported that her early bomb tests revealed an advanced technology. There is no question but that she intends to stand eventually in the first rank of nuclear powers.

2. *Nuclear bombs are becoming cheaper and easier to make.* A proliferation of nuclear powers is a near certainty; not only China but also a score or more countries not now possessing nuclear arms soon may have them.

Added to these two facts is the seldom mentioned one that intercontinental ballistic missiles are not the only available means for the delivery of nuclear weapons. The bomb smuggling and the sudden obliteration of Denver, which are the pivotal events of our scenario, are *present* possibilities. If any one of the nuclear powers wished to smuggle bombs into the United States it is clearly within the realm of possibility that it could do so. And the United States can, and possibly has, done the same thing in other countries.

Furthermore, the safety features and controls which have now been devised for nuclear weapons are not always operative for all weapons at all times. Bombs must be assembled. They must be moved about. They must be inspected. Accidents can occur.

The possibility of accident, the likelihood of smuggling operations, and the almost certain spread of nuclear weapons to countries not now possessing them means that a country committed to a policy of nuclear deterrence has become trapped in contradictions in which there is no way to exercise reasonable responsibility.

Thus war can no longer represent a rational continuation of politics by other means. There is no way to denuclearize war, and scarcely anyone any longer believes there is. There is no way to keep limited war from threatening to become total. There is no way to guarantee that war with conventional arms will not escalate into a nuclear war. Nor does guerrilla war offer an adequate substitute. Mao Tse-tung, the most successful exponent of guerrilla war, has said that "the concept that guerrilla warfare is an end in itself and can be divorced from those of the regular forces is incorrect."[2] If we try to confine our military reliance to guerrilla-type operations, as in counterinsurgency warfare, we are forced by the necessities of such warfare to develop and maintain regular forces also. We have seen how this has worked in Vietnam.

Two possibilities remain. One is a unified world political system in which there is no resort to war. The other is the use of nonviolent means of national defense. The two are not mutually exclusive. In fact, if the first is, at long last, to come about, it depends upon developing the second and putting it into practice.

Two studies which conclude that nuclear deterrence threatens national security have been written by unusually well qualified analysts. The first is *The Demilitarized World* by Walter Millis and the second, *National Security and the Nuclear-Test Ban* by Jerome B. Wiesner and Herbert F. York.

Walter Millis has expressed the belief that the irrelevance of the modern war machinery to the real power conflict is becoming ever more widely acknowledged and will have profound effects.

> The military establishment will progressively decline into forces policing through their defensive roles a more or less established world order; while international politics advances to the generally nonviolent regulation and adjustment of the power struggles that will continue to take place in the world. The threat of war, as it becomes increasingly less credible

---

[2] S. B. Griffith, *Mao Tse-tung on Guerrilla Warfare*, (New York: Praeger, 1962).

and less usable, is bound to become less and less prominent in international affairs; while the questions of whether the enormous costs and even more enormous perils of the super-militarized system cannot be dispensed with is bound to become more urgent.[3]

The study by Wiesner and York analyzes the technical requirements of nuclear deterrence. They declare: "Ever since shortly after World War II the military power of the United States has been steadily increasing. Throughout this same period the national security has been rapidly and inexorably diminishing." They then show that the same is true of the Soviet Union. They conclude with this striking paragraph:

> Both sides in the arms race are thus confronted by the dilemma of steadily increasing military power and steadily decreasing national security. *It is our considered professional judgment that this dilemma has no technical solution.* If the great powers continue to look for solutions in the area of science and technology only, the result will be to worsen the situation. The clearly predictable course of the arms race is a steady open spiral downward into oblivion.[4]

To resolve the dilemma they urge renewed efforts for a comprehensive test ban with inspection.

These two studies agree on the irrelevance of nuclear arms to national purpose and on the desirability of discovering non-violent means of resolving conflict among nations. Both place their hopes on negotiating settlements. Walter Millis is particularly explicit in his expressions of hope that "enough" world government is emerging and will continue to emerge before long to allow for an assembly of nations which will successfully provide administrative resources for the world community, enabling international conflicts to be dealt with and resolved without war. We share these hopes.

---

[3]Published by the Center for the Study of Democratic Institutions, Santa Barbara, Calif., 1964.

[4]*Scientific American,* October, 1964.

Even so, it is difficult for us to see how the attitude of the world conmmunity can be developed to the point where wars among its members are clearly discarded as a part of the system, without a long period of transition and insecurity during which war, including nuclear war, may occur. Although in our own country the Constitution incorporated a system of checks and balances, the fact that seventy-five years later we had a murderous Civil War clearly indicates that the original system was inadequate in the sense that it was not complete and finished, nor could it be finished then and there, all at once. Time had to pass. Procedures had to develop. Relationships had to be tested. Powers had to be established by initiatives and assertions arising out of the context of historical developments. This process led to the Civil War and only when that frightful struggle ended could it be said that the basic Constitutional question raised by the founding fathers had been settled: Is a state free to secede rather than accept overriding federal authority on vital issues? The secession issue has already been raised in the United Nations with the withdrawal of Indonesia in 1965.

If a world authority or a government became tyrannical one nonviolent sanction open to constituent states would be to secede. Other nonviolent sanctions—which preserved the political unity that existed—would obviously be preferable, but it is clear that no pat answer can be given to this problem. Even before the secession issue is finally disposed of there are likely to be bitter and dangerous events, provocations, and conflicts in which neither the United Nations, nor the sense of restraint which the nuclear dilemma has imposed, can be relied upon to assure peace and nonviolent solutions. The differences in language, in culture, in economic systems, in political systems, in economic and political developments, in moral and ethical attitudes and sensitivity, which exist in the world today are much greater than existed among the settlers and the inhabitants of the original thirteen colonies in the 1770's and 1780's. It is reasonable to assume that these differences will make the process of achieving world community much more difficult, more dangerous and probably more time-consuming than the difficulties the colonies faced in developing the federalist community.

It took roughly ninety years, culminating in the Civil War, to settle the issues of federalism which the American Revolution raised. Can today's issues of world community be finally settled in less time? Can they be settled with less hazard of resort to war? We may all hope so, but it does not seem likely. Considering the state of our world today, the idea of world community seems to many pure moonshine. But we may be further along the road then we realize. A brief study by Justice Douglas in *The Rule of Law in World Affairs,* published in 1961 by the Center for the Study of Democratic Institutions, describes the considerable forces and institutions which now operate to make the rule of law a reality among the nations. Justice Douglas concludes with these words:

> War from time out of mind has been one of the remedies for real or fancied wrongs. Now that it is obsolete, the rule of law remains as the only alternative. This is not an expression of hope alone. We have in truth the sturdy roots of a rule of law, including a few of the procedures which human ingenuity has devised for resolving disputes including conciliation and mediation, arbitration, administrative settlement, and judicial determination. The rule of law is versatile and creative. It can devise new remedies to fit international needs as they may arise. The rule of law has at long last become indispensable for nations as well as for men. Now that the instruments of destruction have become so awesome that war can no longer be tolerated, the rule of law is our only alternative to mass destruction.[5]

Justice Douglas hopes that disarmament and the rule of law can move ahead together rapidly enough to forestall nuclear war. That is the essence of the hope which is developed some-

---

[5]William O. Douglas, *The Rule of Law in World Affairs.*

what more fully, as we have mentioned, in Walter Millis' *The Demilitarized World.*

But what if it does not work out that way? What if major conflict comes before world community has matured? How can we cope with major international conflict now? What happens between now and the actual emergence of that world without war which Justice Douglas and Walter Millis, along with the great bulk of mankind, desire?

> *We believe the answer to this question lies in the application of the technique of nonviolent action, developed systematically in accord with a national decision to engage in civilian defense.*

We therefore return to the basic question our scenario suggests: Until the emergence of an adequately matured world community, how does a nation provide for its security in a world where nuclear weapons are being acquired by an increasing number of nations? Even before the Chinese had exploded their bomb on October 16, 1964, Secretary McNamara said in a public radio interview on October 3, 1964:

> "We anticipate in the years ahead because of the advances in nuclear technology, the cost of nuclear weapons will fall dramatically. As it falls, and as the technology becomes simpler, we can expect more and more nations to acquire capability for both developing and producing such weapons. You can imagine the danger that the world would face if ten, twenty, or thirty nations possessed nuclear warheads instead of the four that possess them today."

Our scenario uses a smuggled bomb interception and the unresolved nuclear destruction of a major American city as the final debacle which forces change in defense policy. We do not expect this precise sequence of events to occur, but scenarios of this sort are becoming fairly common today. Such films as "Dr. Strangelove" and "Fail-Safe" have portrayed similar disasters, based not on make-believe but on real factors in our present situation. Although some military experts found these films factually inaccurate, we need to acknowledge the possibility that some such disaster could occur. Doubtless, if a disaster did occur, policy changes would follow. It would become impossible to believe any longer that a world without war could be developed while we continue to rely on nuclear deterrence.

We propose that the country seriously consider *now* what it should do. It is a requirement of survival that we *develop* the essentially human capacity to anticipate the hazards which can lead to our own destruction and *use* this capacity of anticipation to *choose* another course in time. We believe that there still is time. The course that we propose for consideration is the organization of the resources of the country for nonviolent defense.

> *We propose that the United States recast its entire defense effort and rely upon civilian defense based on nonviolent action and thereby do its part in the creation of a world community in which war will no longer have a place.*

2 | Preparation and Training for Civilian Defense

Many people assume that an almost certain result of total disarmament would be the invasion of the United States by an enemy power. The writers of this paper do not concede that invasion would necessarily result. In fact, we consider it highly unlikely. (See Chapter VI for our reasons.) Yet we recognize that any workable defense system must be prepared to cope with such an eventuality, however improbable. Our belief that civilian defense could successfully meet the challenge of an armed invasion stems from (1) historical evidence, which will be briefly considered here, and (2) the theoretical extension of nonviolent techniques to cope with an invasion situation, considered in the next chapter.

The historical instances below bear witness to the potential of nonviolent action for national defense. However, we should point out that these uses of nonviolent methods were not uni-

formly successful, nor were they all entirely unmixed with the
use of violence. In each case the emphasis was on resisting
the invader; nonviolence was the means to an end. In no case
was the nonviolent resistance planned in advance. With advance training and organization, as in civilian defense, we
believe that the efficiency and power of nonviolent techniques
could be greatly increased.

In the Ruhr in 1923 France sent 60,000 troops to protect a
group of technicians who were to take over and run the mines
and plants because Germany was behind in reparations pay-
ments. The German governmental leaders, supported by German industrialists, committed the Ruhr to passive resistance to
the French. The French "were received in silence by an angry
and impotent population. The offices of the mining syndicates
were closed, the great coke and blast furnaces remained idle,
the shops of Essen were barred and shuttered and the blinds
of every window drawn against the invaders. Railwaymen
refused to carry coal from France, policemen refused to remain
on duty rather than salute French officers, youthful enthusiasts
sabotaged signals, points, and telephones, sank barges and
opened locks, and the shopkeepers and restaurant proprietors
refused to serve French soldiers and the girls to speak to
them."[1] For a period of nearly a year resistance of this sort
completely frustrated French efforts to force industrial production.

> The great Krupp von Bohlen and his fellow mine-owning
> magnates were sentenced to enormous fines and long terms of
> criminal imprisonment; mayors and municipal officials were
> arrested and carted off to gaol in lorries; striking workmen
> were whipped, clubbed with rifle-butts and shot down with
> machineguns. In the course of a few months 140,000 humble
> citizens were evicted from their homes for the crime of refus-
> ing to obey French military orders.[2]

---

[1] Arthur Bryant, *Unfinished Victory* (London: Macmillan and Co.,
Ltd., 1940), pp. 124-25.
[2] *Ibid.*, pp. 125-26.

Despite brutality and terror, the Germans held out long enough to force negotiations which ended in a settlement favorable to Germany.

In Finland, during its struggle against Russification from 1899 to 1905, non-cooperation was used by the Finns as a basic strategy. Conscripts refused to serve in the army; officials refused to attach their signatures to papers; judges ignored legislative and executive orders, petitions were circulated, public demonstrations were organized, emigration was encouraged, the clergy preached resistance from their pulpits, and finally in 1905 a general strike was called. The campaign ended in success for the Finns. Innovations ruthlessly forced upon the Finns in an effort to absorb the people into Russia were withdrawn, military conscription was rescinded, and the Finnish Diet was summoned to re-establish constitutional government.[3]

In Denmark during World War II the Germans occupied the country and at first interfered very little with Danish domestic policy, then gradually began to put pressure on the Danes to conform to the Nazi program. This culminated in an effort to launch a characteristic anti-Semitic campaign. King Christian, who as a matter of maintaining national morale during the occupation rode daily through the streets of Copenhagen on horseback, after announcing that he would live in any ghetto that was established and would wear the yellow star of David if Jews were required to wear it, attended a ceremony in a synagogue in full uniform. Later, when an anti-Nazi German attached to the German legation in Copenhagen got word to Danish leaders of a Nazi plan to round up all Jews in Denmark on the night of October 1, 1943, a vast network of resources was brought into play involving Protestant churches, Catholic cloisters, private homes, hotels, farms, taxis, other

---

[3]Sources included J. Hampden Jackson, *Finland* (New York: The Macmillan Co., 1940); William Robert Miller, *Nonviolence: A Christian Interpretation* (New York: Association Press, 1964); John H. Wourinen, *Nationalism in Modern Finland* (New York: Columbia University Press, 1931).

vehicles, and small sailing craft and boats of all kinds to smuggle the Jews to Sweden across the Ore Sound. Some 7,500 escaped in this way and less than 50 were caught.[4]

In the resistance of Hungary to Austria from 1849 to 1867 "passive resistance" was the official policy of the Hungarian Deputies directing the struggle even after they went underground. Tactics included tax refusal and non-cooperation with the auctioning of seized goods, boycott by Hungarian representatives of the Imperial Parliament, social ostracism of the Austrian soldiers billeted with Hungarians, occupation of Council chambers by councilmen until they were forced out, boycott of Austrian goods, and inviting time in jail for selective buying.[5]

As a result of this nonviolent resistance Hungarian nationalism flowered. The governing group remained united and continued to meet throughout the struggle. The action weakened Austria in the face of a war with Prussia. When the Imperial Parliament met without Hungarians present, the Prussian and French press "poked such fun at it that it became a topic of laughter throughout Europe."[6] Finally, the campaign achieved considerable success, bringing the constitution of Hungary back into effect with a high degree of national autonomy.

We conclude from these instances and from others that could be cited, that there is nothing about the nature of government itself which precludes its using nonviolent sanctions as a means of expressing its power.

------

[4]Sources include Hannah Arendt, *Eichmann in Jerusalem* (New York: Viking Press, 1963); Richard Gregg, *The Power of Nonviolence* (Nyack, New York: Fellowship Publications, 1959); Borge Outze, ed., *Denmark during the German Occupation* (Copenhagen: Scandinavian Publishing Co., 1946).

[5]Arthur Griffith, *The Resurrection of Hungary: A Parallel for Ireland* (Dublin: Whelan and Sons, 1918); pp. 1-68 are a selection of Mulford Q. Sibley, ed., *The Quiet Battle* (New York: Anchor Books, 1963), pp. 139-155.

[6]Griffith in Sibley, *op. cit.*, p. 149.

PREPARATION OF THE PEOPLE

The cases of nonviolent action cited above occurred *without* advance preparation of the people for the struggle. It is therefore, all the more surprising that power could be generated under conditions of pressure and intimidation. We believe that the success of these movements shows the potential. An intensive program of national preparation *in advance* of the struggle would multiply considerably the effect that nonviolent resistance could have and would build confidence in Civilian Defense through the following.

1. *Revised concepts of the role of established institutions in national security*

The fact that nuclear arms can no longer provide a means of national defense—the bankruptcy of the nuclear deterrence concept—must be understood. Even today many an "average man-in-the-street" feels instinctively that nuclear weapons cannot really defend—that we are in fact engaged in the suicidal business of preparing to blow ourselves up. This suggests public readiness for policy change.

Tragically, a mood of apathy and accommodation pervades and permeates the nation and the world today; we do little or nothing to halt the arms race and press for an alternative. A United States that had put its reliance in civilian defense would act differently. Not only would it seek an alternative to nuclear suicide, it would act upon the alternative.

The habits of thought and the attitudes engendered by the cold war period and the centuries-old reliance upon armaments require the focusing of attention upon the reasons that necessitate change. This may be brought about through carefully planned speeches by national leaders, including the President himself, by research reports and well-publicized scholarly analyses, by widely shown special films and television programs, and by a host of additional contributions from all the institutions and agencies of our society. Through all these efforts the

bankruptcy of nuclear deterrence and the availability of a
bona fide alternative would be emphasized.

2. *Development of commitment*

A population must be trained if it is to fight nonviolently just
as it is conditioned to fight violently. A nation of saints, however, is not required. There is evidence in nonviolent resistance
movements that a high degree of solidarity and incorruptibility
in the face of the most frightening pressures can in fact be
achieved by ordinary people once they have committed themselves to a cause. During World War II millions of people on
both sides, *having accepted the premises of violent struggle,*
displayed tremendous courage, made great sacrifices and en-
dured unbelievable suffering without yielding to the enemy.
Pattern bombing, far from breaking the will of either the
Germans or Britains, actually strengthened the determination
to resist. On what basis can it be claimed that a people, *having
once accepted the premises of nonviolent struggle,* would be
unable to rise to the same heights of endurance and fortitude?

The second step in preparing for civilian defense is therefore the development of a sense of confidence in the method
of the struggle, springing in part from the genuine solidarity
of the national community. This requires organized preparation and training at both the theoretical and the technical
levels if the country is to be ready for outside attack. The confidence of the nonviolent demonstrators for civil rights in the
United States bears eloquent testimony to the power which
can be released by a struggle with nonviolent weapons. To
duplicate this commitment must be one of the first goals of
realistic preparation for nonviolent defense.

3. *Dramatization of past history, with emphasis on the power exercised by ordinary citizens*

Social struggles in which the power of nonviolent direct
action has played a significant part are dramatic. Their successes and failures invite analysis and discussion. There is so-

cial power on every hand awaiting to be tapped for use in civilian defense: the power exercised by ordinary citizens in the normal course of daily life in typical American communities; the power of the housewife to reassure or arouse the neighborhood; the power of the worker to perform or withhold his work; the power of the clergyman to counsel and encourage his people; the power of the business man to guide productive capacities of the community; the power of the lawyer to project concepts of fairness and justice; the power of the scholar to engage in significant research and analysis; the power of the editor to speak the truth to the community; the power of the entertainer to clothe social courage in bright colors; the power of the creative artist to speak to people at the level of their deepest feelings; the power of music and singing; and the power that the young people have to inspire hope for the future. All of these quite "ordinary" powers will be assessed in local communities committed to civilian defense. People will be encouraged to ask themselves how they can use their abilities to defend the community and hold it together during times of special peril and stress.

A vital factor in resistance movements is the ability of the "average citizen" to be inventive in "spur-of-the-moment" situations where no prior thought or preparations has been possible. Inventiveness and ingenuity in unanticipated situations are needed for effective opposition to an enemy seeking to impose his will upon a people.

Power at best is very fragile and it is always difficult for a government to govern. Its authority rests upon the willingness of the people to obey. Once this willingness disappears the rulers are in a hopeless position. Any government, therefore, must avoid a showdown with the people. In numerous national revolutions the vastly superior material power that rested with the governing authority proved entirely inadequate in the face of deep popular opposition. We need to look no further than our own South for illustrations of the fact that in many situations those in authority become afraid to confront the people's protest, and consequently yield to their demands.

Ordinary people, helped by understanding the methods, nature, and practice of civilian defense, will be able to improvise action which will render impotent the will of an invader. Social meaning can be given to the basic truth: "So long as the citizens remain firm and refuse to cooperate and obey, the real power lies with them . . . . A dictator is no less dependent upon the sources of power granted to him by the subjects than any other ruler, and if those sources of his power can be withheld by . . . non-cooperation and disobedience . . . , then he too will be unable to maintain himself as ruler."[7]

4. *Creating the acceptance of personal responsibility for resistance, with identification of the personal capacities needed*

Civilian defense requires the support and participation of the population even more than does military resistance. While there will be leadership in depth and organized cadres of full-time resisters, the popular support of the people will give the movement its essential power, making it possible to surprise the enemy, and imposing on him an impossible task: to police a whole population, town by town and house by house. "Political activities," wrote General Vo Nguyen Giap, commander of the victorious Viet Minh guerrillas in their campaign against the French, "were more important than military activities . . . . Organization of the masses, carried out everywhere in the country, particularly at key points, was of decisive importance."[8] The same could be said in describing what happened in Algeria. There the French did not lose a military war, they lost only the social struggle. An entire population was marshalled against them, making it impossible to impose their

---

[7]Gene Sharp in Adam Roberts, ed., *Civilian Defense*, (London: Peace News, 1964).

[8]Jerry A. Rose, "The Elusive Viet Cong," in *The New Republic*, May 4, 1963, as quoted by Sidney Lens in *The Futile Crusade—Anti-Communism As American Credo* (Chicago: Quadrangle Books, 1964).

rule under the circumstances of mass defection that occurred. Civilian defense begins at the same point as the guerrilla warfare in Vietnam and Algeria, with popular allegiance strong enough to withstand the pressures that armed intervention by a repressive regime produce.

TRAINING FOR ACTION

As the people come to understand the means of civilian defense and accept their personal responsibility in it, emphasis must also be placed on specific training for action. It should be stressed that this major task will not require the introduction and perfection of a great range of new skills. It rather will involve a re-orientation as to how skills such as those of organization, communication, resistance, and relating constructively to people, can be directed into the strategic and tactical operations of civilian defense.

Although the field of training is vast and relatively unexplored, we are encouraged by pioneering efforts underway in England, Canada, India, Norway, West Germany, Holland and the United States, including the founding of a full-time training institute in the United States for workers engaged in social action with a commitment to nonviolence.[9] Much of this is preliminary, provisional, and experimental, but it *is* being undertaken and its importance increasingly recognized.

All the resources of our society may be mobilized to contribute to the effective training of many people in a variety of ways. As nations have traditionally girded for military defense, putting whatever was required at the disposal of the defense effort, so must the nation gird the civilian defense, holding back nothing deemed essential for the most effective prepara-

---

[9]The Upland Institute, an educational institution developing on the campus of the Crozer-Chester Medical Center and the Crozer Theological Seminary, Chester, Pennsylvania.

tions possible. Television and radio can broadcast instructions to be followed at critical junctures and in emergency situations that may arise at a future date. Classes can be held and training given through these same mass media. Newspapers and magazines can carry articles, lessons, training courses in serial form, all geared to instruct and mobilize the public for effective participation in nation-wide nonmilitary defense. Special civilian defense literature can be published and widely distributed by the government. A number of key institutions and agencies in our society, such as the churches and trade unions, can cooperate in organizing special civilian defense groups, some for the purposes of study and discussion, others to experiment with actual training in skills, methods, and techniques.

Since the most effective training is intimately bound up with action, field work should be organized and supervised. Manuals governing civilian behavior under particular situations can be prepared for general public distribution. Such instructions should prescribe ways in which an invader's military and civilian personnel are to be treated, summarize legal codes to be applied under occupation conditions, give instructions about hiding resisters and defectors from the enemy army, and furnish much other necessary information.

Once a year in many sections of the country a simulated "invasion" might take place so that problems of strategy and tactics can be posed and tested and the whole machinery of civilian defense given a practice run. Though such games would have a quality of unreality about them, the value of such exercises has been indicated by military "war games," and more especially by role-playing employed by the freedom movement to prepare civil rights workers for service in the South. The games could teach basic principles and enable people to discover their own unexpected capacities for working out perplexing problems together. Both ideas for effective action and discovery of problems would emerge, many of which might have been suggested or considered, apart from the simulated situation.[10]

In addition to the general broad training given to the population, intensive programs would be provided for the responsible leadership of the resistance. Their training would include instruction in depth in the philosophy and psychology of nonviolent resistance; study of the history of nonviolent action, its failures as well as its successes, experiences of resistance movements, anti-colonial struggles, strikes, the American civil rights movements, policing and peace-keeping operations, guerrilla efforts, and some types of military actions as well; courses in problems of leadership, organization or economic resources, and the social organization of nonviolent resistance; classes in physical education, and physical fitness drills. The leaders would also engage in language study, and would become acquainted with the customs, culture, and ideology of potential national enemies in order to better understand the feelings and reactions both of troops and populations.

---

[10]An extended experiment in the nonviolent defense of a community, based on the acting out of a socio-drama, was conducted in the summer of 1965 at Grindstone Islands, Canada, sponsored by the Canadian Friends Service Committee and the American Friends Service Committee. A thoroughly documented report on this experiment has been published: Theodore Olson and Gordon Christiansen, *Thirty-one Hours* (Toronto: Canadian Friends Service Committee, 1966).

3 | Organization
and Strategy
of the Resistance

Preparation and training to wage an effective struggle against an invader must be conducted in accordance with the strategic requirements of civilian defense organizational arrangements which best serve these requirements. Here again let us stress that in the event of the United States adopting nonviolent defense we consider an invasion extremely unlikely (see Chapter VI) but we nevertheless accept the possibility that it could occur.

The grand strategy of nonviolent resistance to invasion is based upon selective non-cooperation with the machinery and purposes of the invasion and upon dealing with the invaders as people rather than as a category. In principle, civilian defenders do not surrender or accommodate to the incoming army. They challenge the army's authority by tactics of non-cooperation, and by initiating personal relationships with members of the invasion on terms of their own creation and choice. The aim of civilian defense is not only to resist aggression and tyranny, but to so affect the will of the invader's troops and agents that they become unreliable; for example, they cease carrying out orders efficiently, and give information and other help to the resistance. On central issues the resisters give no ground. At the same time, they realize that the invaders are human beings who may be induced in time to doubt the rightness of the invasion, or even to desert. Thus, civilian defense loosens the ties that bind the invading troops in obedience to the orders of their leaders, rendering the invaders hesitant and insecure.

Though an invasion can be resisted nonviolently with such telling effect that the invader will wish he had never invaded, this does not necessarily mean that he will withdraw. Instead he may intensify his efforts, hoping to avoid both at home and in the eyes of the world the disgrace of being forced to admit defeat at the hands of a nonviolent people. Thus even a defeated invasion might drag on for some time, during which the endurance of the resisters would be sorely tested.

We do not paint a rosy picture. We envision an aggressor against a country that presents absolutely no military threat and is subjected to the severest forms of repression. Civilian defense against such an invasion would result in widespread death and injury to the resisters. The number of casualties could be large, though certainly far less than in the event of a thermonuclear war.

We must be prepared for ruthless reprisals. For example the invader might threaten to wipe out one American city each day by bomb until the leaders of the resistance agreed to surrender. Plans for "strategic surrender" would be made in advance to meet such tactics. The strategy in such a case would be to reduce non-cooperation to a minimum, while possibilities for work slow-downs and "accidents" would remain. Civilian defense leaders would not abandon nonviolent defense, but they would adapt the resistance to the threat of genocide. International aspects of civilian defense in such a case would become increasingly important as the very threat of genocide would be used to isolate the invaders from his usual friends and allies.

Through the constructive use of the diplomatic resources of the invaded country and of other countries, as well as those of the United Nations, an effort could be made to provide the aggressor nation with a "way out" gracefully. The full weight of diplomatic resources of the invaded country, of friendly nations, and of those neutral in the dispute would seek to bring the United Nations and other international agencies to bear in effecting a settlement. It will be for the U.N. to assert the conscience of mankind in the situation, to provide a forum where the issues can be identified and dealt with in a corporate way, assuming from the start that when the conflict has been settled each party to the dispute will still have a place in the world which it can accept without disgrace or humiliation.

Civilian direct action methods would also be possible, such as stimulating protest in the invader's country by such methods as droping leaflets from planes to describe the brutality of the invaders against a peace-seeking people, or by an international peace walk into the invader's country.

THE INVASION

Civilian defense depends upon sustained contact and, therefore, is not based upon physical defense of terrain, area by area. It would sacrifice geographical defense because its resources are not really effective for a stand at the border.[1] Border stands tend to be unreal in civilian defense, because of both the ease of by-passing the resisters and the absence of sustained interaction between human beings, which is the key to the effectiveness of civilian defense. Even so, geography

---

[1]In this day of orbiting satellites and intercontinental missiles, of supersonic aircraft and submarine infiltration, borders are not kept inviolate with weapons of war.

will play a role for civilian defense in other respects. The invader will probably be less interested in occupying rural areas than urban centers. In a stretch of country as vast as the United States the invader would not be able to go everywhere —many unoccupied areas would provide staging and command areas for the resistance.

Although, in civilian defense, defense *at* a border may not be possible, defense *of* a border is—defense of the ideas and the way of life that start at the border. It will be important to make clear to invading troops by symbolic border opposition and by saturation announcements that the invasion is unwelcome, unjust, and unnecessary. An offer should be made to settle real grievances of the invading country once the invasion is withdrawn. It will also be important to make clear to invading troops that they are in no physical danger from the civilian defense forces. This places on them the onus of any harm done to the civilian population. At the same time, the civilian defenders should not minimize the possibility of uncontrollable, spontaneous, acts of violent retaliation from an outraged population if the invaders fail to take popular sentiment into account.

> Civilian defense requires, therefore, that the population realize that in case of invasion the country will be initially occupied. The civilian defenders must make invading troops realize that they are intruders whose presence is not justified. Civilian defense strategy is geared to personal confrontation between those who are defending their lives and values and those who would take them away. Military strategy places such importance on the power to invade that it wins geographic victories at the price of making over people into the image of the enemy. Nonviolent defense proposes to reverse this process. It allows invasion of the national soil or territory temporarily in order that the defense of its values and its way of life may be directly pursued, engaging the invaders as *persons* and engaging the invading regime directly as the enemy attempts to use military and political power to control the population and alter the way of life of the country.

Civilian defense against occupation has its strong points which both compare and contrast with military defense. On the one hand, hatred and desire for revenge resulting from fierce fighting and devastation are not factors. Neither side is whipped into frenzy by mass slaughter, either given or received. The bonds of common humanity are thus more easily asserted. On the other hand, open and avowed resistance, is undertaken. Though occupied, the invaded nation is *not* ipso facto defeated. Its people are not compliant. They have not surrendered. Collaboration between the invader and the occupied population is thus less likely than in traditional military invasions.

SELECTIVE NATURE OF THE RESISTANCE

The application of non-cooperation in civilian defense under most conditions would be a selective rather than a total attempt to thwart and paralyze the invader. While theoretically effective, the complete and continuous refusal to operate the industries most vital to the invader's productive occupation (the key transportation systems, the public utilities, and the government services) would be difficult in practice to implement and sustain. At a point when the morale of the invader has been sufficiently lowered and he is sufficiently disorganized, total non-cooperation may be used by the resisters to bring about the final collapse of the invader's regime and hasten his withdrawal. But prior to this stage, selective non-cooperation should be applied.

The strategy of selective non-cooperation would involve calling and terminating strikes and resistance at key points in accordance with timetables set in advance or scheduled by leadership in the course of the struggle on the basis of civilian morale, enemy actions, or other strategic considerations. Thus, today there may be a strike at a Gary steel mill, tomorrow a slowdown at a Camden shipyard, next week a crippling transportation halt in San Francisco and, just as that nears its end, a frustrating railroad commutation tie-up in the New York metropolitan area. Where will the invader look next for the disruption that may just as likely not take place?

The strategy of selective non-cooperation, with the implied threat of possible general strike and total non-cooperation ever present, would constitute the basis of civilian defense on the economic front. A population trained in the use of these methods and acting with determination, would frustrate the economic aims of the invader. Not even tens of thousands of imported technicians could keep the American economy going! Not only would they have to be trained to operate complex economic processes, they would also have to possess the language to work in an economy still manned mostly by Americans. The plain fact is that no nation or group of nations could spare enough highly qualified technicians from work in their own country to perform such a task successfully.

Resistance activity would be focused on defense of national independence, keying action to the maintenance of freedom of speech, of a democratic society, of opposition to indoctrination and any attempts to fragment social cohesion. Initiative must always be retained and used by the resister; he must use it with imagination and flexibility whether in crisis stages which may call for a general strike or during the long range period of selective non-cooperation.[3]

THE REQUIREMENT OF OPENNESS

In addition to being non-geographic in character and selective in application civilian defense is essentially open rather than secretive. As a matter of practical necessity to maintain morale, secretiveness and sabotage is the exception, rather than

---

[3]An interesting variant of selective nonviolence has been suggested by a military officer consultant to the working party. He proposed that the resisting people might operate the country on a sort of "limited basis," with partial production and partial services. He compared this approach to the slowdown in labor disputes where sufficient cooperation is withheld to create great difficulties for the employer.

the rule. Herein lies a principle difference between civilian defense and guerrilla warfare; the latter relies heavily on secrecy
and sabotage, the former on openness and non-cooperation. In
a guerrilla operation, for example, a troop train is wrecked by
dynamiting the track; in nonviolent defense the troop movement will be impeded by refusal to fuel or operate the train
or perhaps by resisters who stand *en masse* on the rails in
front of the train. But the civil defenders will not take action
which directly threatens life; nor will they make stealth a
virtue when it is employed as a necessity.

A leading Norwegian member of his country's resistance to
the Germans in World War II has said that resistance against
the Nazis was best and most effective when it was open. Some
students of the resistance in Denmark during the same period
feel that sabotage hurt the movement by provoking bloody
reprisals. Sabotage is a two-edged sword that may do more
to hurt the resistance than to help it. As Captain Liddell Hart,
the eminent British military analyst, has pointed out, an occupying army sometimes welcomes sabotage as an opportunity
to justify the use of large-scale repression. Baffled by the nonviolent character of the resistance, the invader's general staff
might see sabotage as close enough to violence to justify a
campaign of terror.

We find it impossible to be purists regarding secrecy and
sabotage. Further research and experimentation are required
to determine whether they are *ever* called for in civilian defense. Some authorities believe that any use of secrecy or sabotage would inevitably weaken nonviolent defense by provoking fear in the invader and causing and justifying reprisals.
Bradford Lyttle points out that such tactics "justify the real-
izations which give one's opposition his moral and determination to employ force and violence. They discourage in him
the processes of thought and reflection that will lead him to
doubt the rightness of his cause. They sustain the image of
alienness, hostility, and malevolence which he has of you. They
prevent the resisters from assuming a prophetic and redemp-

tive role, in other words, from challenging the philosophic principles from which violence and aggression flow."[4]

We feel that the justification for secrecy is most compelling in cases where men who are in hiding are likely to be executed by the invaders if apprehended. To prevent communications among the defenders from breaking down, clandestine newspapers and radio stations are often thought to be necessary. Some feel that sabotage is justified when one is able to destroy weapons or ammunition of the invaders. Should the acknowledged leaders of civilian defense be killed or otherwise incapacitated, some suggest that the names of new leaders be kept secret, and though the very nature of nonviolent defense might make this impossible, their whereabouts would probably need to be kept secret.

A general rule of thumb about sabotage might be that it is always immediately ruled out if injury or danger to enemy life is probable. Secrecy and sabotage are dangerous instruments, to be used sparingly, if at all, by civilian defenders. Involvement in this kind of game against the enemy can lead to being made over into their image thereby falling prey to the very qualities which the defenders oppose.

INFLUENCING MEMBERS OF THE INVADING ARMY

One of the objectives of civilian defense will be to exert influence over members of the invading forces through association in a variety of ways with citizens of the invaded community. Efforts will be made to engage enemy soldiers in conversations in which they will be asked why they have come, why they have invaded a nation committed only to civilian defense, what they hope to gain from aggression, and whether

---

[4]This quotation is from Bradford Lyttle's comments on an earlier draft of this paper. He is the author of a pioneer study in the field of civilian defense, *National Defense through Nonviolent Resistance* (Chicago: Shan-ti Sena Publications, 1958).

they understand how their behavior appears in the eyes of the
rest of the world. Nor is all this as fantastic as some might at
first assume it to be. During the Kapp putsch in 1920 irate
citizens made their way into the barracks in Berlin and confronted the soldiers directly, urging on them the wrongness of
what they were doing. This example can be developed into a
widely used tactic. Invader troops must be told daily, directly,
to go home.[5]

Contacts with occupation troops can, of course, and often
do go beyond the level of conversation and argument to a
deeper, more personal level. Even in a country conquered after
a long and horrendous struggle, as in World War II, where
there was great hatred on both sides, where the slaughter and
devastation was unspeakable, where the occupying armies entered full of hatred and desire for revenge, where there was
raping, looting, and wholesale destruction by the troops—even
in such situations, fraternization between soldiers and citizens
begins to develop. Before long the high command of the occupying army has a morale problem on its hands. Attempts are
made to prevent and outlaw fraternization, but eventually
such efforts prove fruitless. In time soldiers are marrying girls
from the conquered nation, and children are being born whose
parents but a short time before were mortal enemies. Contacts
with people of the invaded country have broken down the attitudes of hostility which war generates. In civilian defense
where deliberate and conscious effort is made to establish understanding and communication with invading soldiers by
emphasizing the common humanity which binds occupier and
occupied, these contacts become a phase of the struggle to
conquer the invader.

Through such personal contacts, as well as through public
demonstrations, privately circulated articles and speeches, and
in other ways the members of the invading force will be en-

---

[5]Language study must obviously form an important part of civilian
defense training.

couraged to question the invasion and to consider sympathetically the civilian defense struggle. This will not usually mean defection for the invasion force. It may mean that men would continue to work within the occupation army to influence their colleagues. They would not be expected to renonuce their basic loyalty to their own country, but rather to raise questions about the purposes of the invasion and to refuse any longer to accept the validity of its aims. Lest this appear to be far-fetched, we recall East Germany in June, 1953, when eighteen Soviet soldiers refused to obey the order to fire upon the non-violent demonstrators and were court-martialed and shot. In time troops, surrounded by a population nonviolently resisting their presence, may lose heart and refuse to continue the occupation.

Some members of the invading force are likely to become sympathetic to the defenders more readily than others. Thus, divisions of opinion will develop, adversely affecting invader morale and efficiency. The invaders, for their part, can be expected to use their own propaganda techniques to try to maintain the morale of their troops and to destroy the morale of the resisters. They are certain to try to control the mass media. Frequent troop rotation can also be expected. Contact between the troops and the defenders will be controlled and dehumanized as much as possible. However, considerable person-to-person contact is unavoidable. This is likely to be the most potent weapon in the civilian defender's arsenal.

WINNING SUPPORT OF NONALIGNED COUNTRIES

Political work with nonaligned countries must begin in advance. Much will depend on whether bystander countries refuse to supply economic resources to the invader either through trade or by other means; whether they make diplomatic expressions of disapproval, protest, and moral censure; whether they enlist the resources of the United Nations and of other international agencies to get the invasion withdrawn. The fact of invasion will confront nonaligned countries with a threat to their own security unless the world community can bring invasion to an end. Invasion thus will tend to generate powerful forces of unity among the bystanders in confronting the invader and in support of the victim country.

The possibilities of significant bystander support for an invaded country may be seen in the allied invasion of Russia in 1919 and 1920. During the invasion and occupation of parts of Russia supporters of the Russian revolution were active in France and England speaking of their hopes for a new and more abundant life as well as for peace if the revolution should succeed. The Russian revolution captured the imagination of many intellectuals and members of the laboring class who wanted the Russians to have a fair chance to fulfill their hopes and aspirations.

As a result of these efforts, when the French government dispatched five cruisers to the Baltic as part of its anti-Russian effort "the sailors of these ships struck against war. They were brought home in disgrace but they had spiked the guns of the French navy so far as that crusade was concerned."[6]

> Of immeasurably greater import was the prevention of a British war against Russia in 1920. The Cabinet fire-eaters were determined on joining openly in the warfare which they had been carrying on covertly by the aid of the subsidized White armies in new Russia. There was a conscription bill up in Parliament at the time, and this added fuel to the mounting flames of Labor revolt. The Triple Alliance made up of the Railwaymen, the Miners, and the Transport workers, served notice on the government that it demanded the recall of the conscription project, the withdrawal of all British troops in Russia, the release of all conscientious objectors still imprisoned, and the raising of the infamous blockade, which had brought useless and untold agony to a war-destitute peo-

---

[6]Devere Allen, *The Fight for Peace* (New York: Macmillan, 1938) p. 633.

ple. A joint conference of the Labor Party, the Parliamentary Labor Party, and the Trades Union Congress explicitly warned the authorities that "the whole industrial power of the organized workers will be used to defeat this war." The war was defeated; the prestige of the Labor groups was enhanced rather than diminished . . . .[7]

Civilian defense, internationally as well as at home, will constitute a very important aspect of the entire resistance, and will be essential to the maintenance of confidence and morale among special civilian defense forces as well as general population.[8]

INFLUENCING THE INVADER'S PEOPLE

An armed invasion against a peace-seeking nation that posed no military threat would raise inevitable questions with which the invading regime would be forced to deal. Resistance within the invader's country is likely to affect the invasion of a country employing civilian defense as much as anything that happens in the invaded country. Doubtless in some cases invasion of a civilian defense country will end the tyrant's regime at home as well as his power abroad.

Repudiation of the invasion by the people of the invader's country will depend in part upon communicating the reality of the invasion to the people. In a totalitarian state this would not be easy, but such repression inevitably kindles discontent, however deeply hidden. The full diplomatic resources of the invaded country, its allies, nonaligned nations, and international organizations would be brought to bear. Direct action methods, such as leafleting from planes, have already beeen suggested. Franklin Zahn, an American exponent of nonviolent action, points out that such technological advances can be utilized as printing leaflets on paper that sticks to whatever it

---

[7]*Ibid.*

[8]See pages 51 ff.

touches and cannot easily be removed. Short wave radio can also be used to spread the truth.

Here again the problem of secrecy arises. Would nonviolent *agents provocateurs,* stirring the flames of discontent in the invader's country, be warranted in civilian defense? No easy answer is possible. The previously mentioned international peace march into the invader's country by persons willing to face death rather than be stopped would perhaps satisfy the requirements of civilian defense, yet this too can be thwarted by swift, stern arrests and indefinite arbitrary detention.

Here we should point out that one of the main ways in which a government persuades its people to accept arbitrary domestic restrictions is through instilling fear of foreign enemies. When a major nation adopts a civilian defense policy it will be more difficult for opposing nations to justify heavy military expenditures and strict controls. The people will tend to demand that economic resources be used to raise their standard of living. They are likely to demand and gain increasing freedom. Civilian defense can thus spread from people to people.

COMMUNICATION

An invader can be counted on to seize control of all media of communication. This poses a most serious problem for civilian defenders.

Important facts about civilian defense resistance, such as the news of successes and reverses, the suffering of the people, the harshness of the invader, the instructions to the population to maintain discipline and to boost morale—all these and more must be communicated to the general population and to the world. This is highly essential if the resistance is to continue, if the population is to maintain its morale, and if the weight of world opinion and supporting action is to be mobilized. A well-staffed and well-equipped mobile communications system, organized and throughly trained in clandestine operations and supplied by scattered caches of communications eqiupment must a part of civilian defense preparations. People must be recruited and trained for underground courier duty to reinforce and supplement the communications network. Of all arguments for secrecy in the conduct of civilian defense, those in the area of communications are among the strongest. However, such secrecy should not be resorted to automatically. An attempt should be made first to maintain the normal communications system in defiance of the invader.

RANGE OF METHODS AVAILABLE TO RESISTERS

The American student of civilian defense, Gene Sharp, has catalogued and classified methods or forms of action available to civilian defense. These could become the "arsenal" of any government planning to base its defense on nonviolent action. He has identified one hundred and twenty-four forms which civilian defense might take, based on a study of the actual uses of these various methods in historic situations.

The Sharp list is divided into three main divisions which he designates (1) Nonviolent Protest; (2) Nonviolent Non-Cooperation; and (3) Nonviolent Intervention. Under nonviolent protest he lists thirty-six forms of activity including parades, vigils, meetings, and emigration. Under nonviolent non-cooperation he lists seventy-two forms of action in three sub-categories: strikes, boycotts, and political non-cooperation. Under nonviolent intervention he lists sixteen forms of action including sit-ins, hunger strikes, nonviolent obstruction, raids, and parallel government.[8]

Each of the forms of nonviolent action listed by Gene Sharp has been tested in actual situations and has yielded influence and power. Most of them could be used in an infinite variety

---

[8]From Gene Sharp, *The Methods of Nonviolent Action*, an appendix to his Civilian Defense Study Conference paper, *Tactics, Methods and Related Aspects of Resistance* (1964). Originally made available in duplicated form by the Institute for Social Research, Oslo, and to be incorporated in Sharp's forthcoming book, *The Politics of Nonviolent Action*.

of ways and could be applied to a great variety of situations. Each constitutes a genuine exercise of force which, if invoked, would confront the adversary with a problem of power.

STRUCTURAL CONSIDERATIONS: ORGANIZING THE ACTION

1. *Levels of responsibility*

Basic to the organization of effective civilian defense is an understanding of the different levels of resistance responsibility. Here there will be certain organizational parallels with guerrilla war, its core groups, its irregulars, and its suporting population. In civilian defense we envisage (1) a leadership group; (2) a body of trained volunteers, most of them part-time; and (3) behind both a sympathetic population that shelters, informs, and responds to orders.

Leadership of civilian defense may not be committed to nonviolence as a way of life. Though in Denmark during World War II the King was the resistance leader, in most cases nonviolent leaders have not held political power but have risen spontaneously because of the people's response to their capacity for effective leadership. Bradford Lyttle asserts that if Gandhi had lived and India had adopted civilian defense, Gandhi, not Nehru, would have become its leader in an invasion; if Alabama adopted nonviolent defense, Martin Luther King, Jr. not Governor Wallace nor Al Lingo, would become the leader. Even so Martin Luther King was not entirely clear on his commitment to nonviolence as a philosophy when he first assumed leadership in the Alabama civil rights struggle. His commitment to a philosophy of nonviolence grew and deepened as the struggle developed.

Leaders committed to nonviolence in principle would be less likely to forsake civilian defense and resort to violent tactics under severe pressure. However, civilian defense is based upon confidence in nonviolent methods, rather than upon belief in nonviolence in principle. Other qualities of leadership such as imagination, understanding of the situation, judgment of strategy and tactics, and creativity might prove to be more important to civilian defense leadership than commitment to nonviolence in principle. Even so, their sustained hold on the imagination of their followers would depend to a high degree on their capacity to inspire confidence in moral commitment to the basic principles of civilian defense as contrasted with military defense.

The second level would be trained volunteers to coordinate civilian defense in a school, in the factory or business where they worked, or in the neighborhood where they lived. They would be similar to the irregulars of the guerrilla army who "fight by night and bake by day." These men, women, and perhaps children will be couriers to assist in coordinating a variety of tasks and operations, will take part in and stimulate demonstrations and other similar actions, and will use their own inventiveness and ingenuity to find countless ways in which the invader's occupation can be thwarted. Such persons might or might not accept nonviolence in principle, though all, of course, would be committed to the technique of civilian defense.

The third level of responsibility could be that of the supporting population—the "water" through which the "fish" (hard-core resisters) move. Theirs would be the task of occasional participation in mass action—large scale strikes, for example—and of bearing the brunt of day-to-day interaction with the invaders. Here a line must be drawn between friendly fraternization with the enemy aimed at assisting the nonviolent defense effort, and harmful, actually traitorous, collaboration. To keep fraternization within the context of the resistance effort and to prevent it from developing in some cases into a form of collaboration will be difficult, but not impossible.

2. Leadership organization and line of succession

There are undoubtedly various ways in which the advance training and preparation can be organized. The way suggested here is only one of several possibilities. The country could be divided into specific defense areas, which could then be divided into state and local community subdivisions. The governors of the states in each defense area, in consultation with the Secretary of Civilian Defense, might be charged with the selection of an Area Director of Civilian Defense. These Area Directors could well be responsible to the Secretary of Civilian Defense and each could have under him state and community directors appointed by the governors of the states in consultation with other elected officials.

Insofar as possible, general categories of civilian defense strategy and tactics would be explored and selected nationally but the phasing in any particular area could be left up to the local defense directors. Everything would be predicated on the assumptions that communication would be difficult and often impossible, that at times leadership would disappear, and that there would be instances of betrayal.

The role of the central authorities, generally speaking, would probably not be to assume direct command over local civilian defense efforts, but to indicate the type of action to be pursued in any particular locality at a given time, leaving to the local leadership actual control of the action. For instance, Civilian Defense Strategic Category One might include fairly nonprovocative acts of resistance, such as, delegations of petitioners to the invading authority protesting the conduct of the invading forces; sermons by ministers of religion all dealing with a common theme with obvious relevance to the occupation regime, such as that suggested by the Sixth Commandment, "Thou Shalt Not Kill"; silent vigils participated in by large numbers of people of all ages in public places for limited periods of time. Methods in this category would be chosen to involve large numbers of people, convey clear disapproval of the occupation to the authorities, indicate the height of civilian morale, yet not necessarily provoke strong repressive measures.

The categories of strategies could be scaled all the way up to Category Ten, which would include acts of strong and direct interference with the invader, who would be forced either to crush such acts, thereby creating martyrs, or else tolerate them, thus weakening his own position. Included in Category Ten could be such acts as the nonviolent occupation of the offices or other facilities of the invading force; nonviolent obstruction of essential processes of the enemy army, by such means as massing in front of vehicles and refusing to move; sustained mass demonstrations at the headquarters of the invader with demands for evacuation; general strike or total noncooperation.

If permitted to function, the President and his advisers could decide which categories of resistance strategy would be invoked in what areas and for what periods of time. Otherwise, this would be a primary responsibility of the civilian defense central authority who would decide to step up the pace or to ease the pressure, depending upon evaluation of the situation, of enemy morale, citizen morale, and the impact of the mutual interaction upon both invader and invaded.

To maintain leadership in the face of the arrest or execution of the President or other key officials the preparatory program would provide for someone ready to step in as a replacement. This would apply throughout the entire leadership structure. Precisely at this point of succession of leadership civilian defense will face one of its most severe tests. It will not be possible to announce in advance what the succession of leadership should be. To do so would expose the entire organization to attack. Nor would it be possible to hold elections to choose new leadership. Therefore, it may be most practical for each leader to discuss with his immediate peers who his successor should be and in light of this discussion for him to appoint the man of his choice. Each new man upon assuming leadership would then make it his first order of business to name his successor.

In this way there would always exist, in addition to those in office at any given time, a parallel or "shadow" government ready to become active at a moment's notice. *No matter how great the provocation, a government should never resign or abdicate. By not resigning, the indigenous government remains the legitimate government, and thus any government the enemy might appoint is illegal and vulnerable per se.*

3. Discipline and morale

Breaches of discipline must be dealt with not in a haphazard way, but by a legal code drawn up for the duration of civilian defense against invasion. Some quislings are bound to arise. Sanctions against the use of violence in confronting the invader must be clear. Breakdown at this point could seriously jeopardize the whole civilian defense system. The questions involved here are extraordinarily difficult. What sort of sanctions would be suitable against collaborators under civilian defense? What sanctions could or should be used against those defenders who resort to violence under pressure? How could civilian defense courts operate in an occupied country? We will not attempt to deal with these problems here, but will only point out that in this area research and development are greatly needed.

Morale is as crucial for civilian defense as Napoleon recognized it to be for military conflict. The evidence from the Finnish struggle against Russia and the Norwegian struggle against the Germans indicates that there is a great deal of strength to be drawn from the fact that the resister is acting in harmony *with* the national consensus. In this sense civilian defense is quite different from a protest movement. Rather than acting against the weight of his society, the resister will be reinforced—and even pushed—by the force of sentiment from his fellow-citizens. Under such conditions morale will be high; and every sign of victory, such as the rotation of troops or the closing of yet another non-cooperating institution, will give fresh impetus to the movement for liberation.

Richard B. Gregg, author of the pioneering work on nonviolent action, writes:

> Nonviolent resistance operates . . . to end and clear away social defects, economic mistakes, and political errors. The

semi-military discipline of the resisters, the getting rid of bad habits, the learning to struggle without anger, the social unity developed, the emphasis on moral factors, the appeal to the finest in the spirit of the opponents and onlookers, the generosity and kindness required—all these constitute a social purification, a creation of truer values and actions among all concerned. If the struggle involves many people and lasts a long time, the discussions of the issues become so widespread, intense, and detailed that much that was previously hidden or misunderstood is revealed and made clear to all. It is a period of great public education.[9]

However hard experience with ruthless dictatorships may temper the appealing optimism of these words, they still express truths which must be taken into account in any realistic assessment of power.

THE NEED FOR MORE STRATEGIC THINKING

Although we have sketched here several aspects of civilian defense strategy and tactics, we are well aware that there is much more to be done. The military strategists base their work on volumes of case studies, extensive military histories, war games, and other such aids which have not yet been developed for civilian defense.

Extensive research needs to be done, especially in these fields:

1. Resistance movements, including guerrilla warfare, to discover what lessons might be learned that are applicable to the waging of a civilian defense struggle;

2. Nonviolent movement, whether for independence from an outside power or for the establishment of freedom and justice within a nation, again with a view to learning what is relevant for civilian defense efforts;

---

[9]*The Power of Nonviolence.* Revised edition (Nyack, N.Y.: Fellowship Publications, 1959), pp. 86-87. Originally published 1935.

3. Military occupations of defeated countries, to study carefully how both the occupier and the occupied behave; how hostility develops or abates; what causes the rise and fall of troop morale; how troops respond to ostracism on the one hand, to friendliness on the other; what factors stiffen or lessen the popular resistance to the invader; and a host of related questions, answers to which would be invaluable in planning strategy for civilian defense.

Case material is needed. Scenarios must be developed positing a variety of situations, and weighing and evaluating a number of possible responses. We have considered here only an all-out invasion. The need to develop civilian defense strategies against limited forms of invasion is also apparent. How could off-shore fishing rights, for example, be protected nonviolently? Or what if a foreign power launched an armed attempt to seize the gold at Fort Knox or airlifted in workers and technicians to take over uranium mines in Arizona?

Once nonviolent defense had become official government policy, scenarios would be used by civilian defense instructors in much the same way as military leaders today employ scenarios to teach battle strategy and to solve military problems. Moreover, as fairly plausible invasion scenarios are worked out, the process of developing tactics designed to meet the situation at the community level should begin, and should prove to be an absorbing and stimulating experience.

Scenarios ought to be focused on particular problems as well as on broad situations. How will we in our plant meet situation X to achieve goal Y? How will trade unions prepare members to operate in the situation? What plans must be made for continuity of management in the plant? What will churches do? How will we act in our neighborhood? Scenario-discussion of this kind will be essential. Out of these explorations will develop a body of doctrine on which to base the civilian defense effort. Such work, study, and research obviously requires the best skills and brains in the country, and large sums of money for adequate financing. A nation which is seriously considering civilian defense would find both the talent and the money necessary, and would put both to work.

Civilian defense is far more reliant upon the understanding acceptance and active support of the general population than is military defense. In this sense it is more democratic. Furthermore, for civilian defense to be accepted as a national policy, such support and unity must be mustered well in advance, in the absence of such an immediate threat as an impending invasion. Through education and the people's natural willingness to follow respected leaders, an administration such as that suggested in the scenario could probably prepare most of the people to accept civilian defense. Those who could not be persuaded present perhaps the most difficult problem of transarmament to civilian defense. If the armed forces were to be dissolved, officers and men who took it to be their "patriotic duty" to oppose such a policy would present grave dangers, especially while they retained control of the weapons. An attempted coup would be likely. In the event of an invasion after transarmament, violent resisters such as the Minutemen could endanger the whole nonviolent defense effort. While we have no pat answers to these problems, we see no reason to assume they are insoluble. Here again, research and development are needed. We continue to believe that the problems civilian defense poses are less grave than the problem involved in the continuation of the present United States defense policy.

4 | Civilian Defense: Strategic Considerations

The purpose of civilian defense is to defend. It is not an exercise in moral speculation, but a practical means of national defense. Its validity depends upon the degree to which it would meet the following tests as compared with defense based upon military means:

1. Would it provide a rational means of defense in case of attack?

2. Would it contribute to the development of a foreign policy less provocative to potential enemies and more reassuring to friends than a military-based foreign policy?

3. Would it encourage the development of world community in which institutions and processes of security would be a part of the structure and the normal pattern of international relations?

The world today is in a state of dynamic tension and flux. The old colonial empires have now been nearly liquidated, leaving in their place newly independent nations which must develop new political structures and capacities, revise and recast their economic institutions and relationships, and play a role of great potential influence and power in the United Nations and other world bodies. The nations of Europe are in the process of welding a new economic union which, if successful, may constitute an economic power block rivalling in capacity and power the Soviet Union on the one hand and the United States on the other. The appeal of Communism has slackened in the West because of the prosperity of the non-Communist countries, the growing demand within the Communist countries for greater freedom for the expression of diverse opinion, the persistent economic problems of the Soviet Union and its allies, and of the Soviet Union's use of power to enforce control and uniformity. The latter belies the optimistic expectation for the withering away of the state and the end of dictatorship promised in Marxist theory.

The United States has become something of an enigma both to itself and to the rest of the world. Despite the vast military and economic power which its system of political and industrial organization has generated, it seems uncertain and fumbling in the use of power. Military commitments are made which are irrelevant to the problems they are intended to solve. The U.S. moralizes on the one hand about the commitment of the Commmunist system to totalitarianism and violence, and on the other hand uses its vast capacity for violence to maintain dictators in power in Southeast Asia and South America. This enhances the appeal of Communism and smooths the way for Communist leaders in these countries. Even non-Communist leaders working for social change are forced to turn toward Communism in despair of getting help from the United States against large landowners and military juntas interested primarily in their own wealth and power. At the same time, the United States sends vast quantities of economic equipment and supplies and large teams of technicians to help raise the living standards of the people. Yet aid rarely becomes fully effective in terms of human need because of the reactionary political structures which the United States protects, supposedly as a bulwark against Communism.

What the Soviet Union has lost in terms of ideological dynamic it seems to have regained, at least to some extent, through its technological achievements as typified and dramatized by its space explorations. Its success in urbanization and in providing a gradually improved standard of living contributes to its internal stability, and to the desire to avoid war and achieve peaceful co-existence with the United States.

China, however, has moved in to occupy the seat of Marxist revolutionary dedication which the Soviet Union has to a degree relinquished. Regardless of the relative merits of the attacks the Soviet Union and China have been leveling at each other, there is no question but that these two vast Communist countries, one already a super-power and the other rapidly on the road toward becoming one, are engaged in a bitter rivalry for the leadership of the Communist countries which is rooted not only in national pride but also in their differing situations:

China's need to maintain tight revolutionary discipline, and the Soviet Union's need to relax social control;

China's willingness to press issues around her border by military means if necessary, and the Soviet Union's desire for peaceful co-existence;

The Soviet Union's need to modify control commitments around the European border, and China's need to press border and peripheral territorial claims until there is stabilization of her hegemony, particularly in areas such as Taiwan which all Chinese consider to be a part of China.

China's need to gain an acknowledged place in the community of nations, and the Soviet Union's need to maintain leadership over the Communist bloc in the United Nations.

All of these factors have contributed to the rivalry between two great Communist states, and now have produced an intense antagonism which may persist despite the powerful forces influencing them in the direction of reconciliation and cooperation set in motion by American military operations in Vietnam.

The brief recital of these basic trends now at work in the world is enough to remind us that the nuclear age is being ushered in not only with the explosion of nuclear tests, but to the accompaniment of revolutionary political and technological changes which challenge all of man's energies if civilization itself is to survive.

It is out of the context of these changes—changes in weaponry, changes in the technology of economic production, and changes in the conditions under which governments may retain the capacity to govern—that our analysis of the relevance of civilian defense to foreign policy must develop, and it must stand or fall accordingly.

A RADICALLY DIFFERENT FOREIGN POLICY

Foreign policy based on civilian defense would be radically different from foreign policy based on military defense. The goals would be different, the techniques would be different, and the relationships would be different. Stated in general terms the goal of foreign policy based upon military defense in the nuclear age is to maintain military pre-eminence if it has been achieved, and to achieve it if it has not. Nearly all of the great alliances (NATO, SEATO, Warsaw Pact, etc.) are essentially military alliances. To maintain military advantage, the dominant powers extend or withhold trade and economic assistance, gather intelligence, encourage or discourage various kinds of exchange, and underwrite scientific and industrial research and development.

It was once true that war was an extension of foreign policy, a continuation of politics by other means. Today the relationship between policy and weaponry, between politics and war, has been reversed. Today policy is shaped to a significant degree by the requirements of weapons development and use.

The task of developing modern weapons systems is so vast, absorbing so large a part of national resources and energies, and dominating so completely the public sector of national life, that it predetermines the character of response to international problems assuring basic reliance on military solutions.

Politics no longer decides which wars will be fought, but the wars that are fought or threatened determine predominant political relationships. United States policy towards China today is a hard policy of military containment, though there is little or no evidence to support the proposition that China's capacity to extend her influence among the impoverished people of Asia, Africa, and even Latin America is impeded by a show of nuclear force by the United States either in the Bay of Tonkin or in the Caribbean Sea. Indeed our China policy may enhance rather than inhibit China's prestige.

In civilian defense it would be possible at last to reverse the relationship between politics and war. Civilian defense would be an extension of politics. More accurately, it would carry the methods of politics into the heart of conflict itself. Defense could be based on new foreign policies consistent with the concepts of civilian defense. A nation which had decided to rely on nonmilitary methods of defense because they were more rational and effective than nuclear deterrence, would free itself and its foreign policy from the iron vice of nuclear determinism.

THE GOALS OF CIVILIAN
DEFENSE FOREIGN POLICY

Today the goals of American foreign policy have been vulgarized by an almost single-minded preoccupation with containing Communist expansion and neutralizing Communist influence, supporting nations pitted in conflict against Communism, and winning as many nations as possible to our side in the struggle between East and West, relying basically on nuclear deterrence to accomplish these ends. Civilian defense would transform the goals and the methods of foreign policy.

Policies toward Communist countries, toward other western nations, and toward the new nations and the nonaligned would be keyed to establishing security relationships and solving problems nonmilitarily. Instead of military containment the major emphasis would be on removing the conditions which encourage Communism and its obdurate and fanatical attitudes, pressing Communist countries into tight alliances of defense against hostile anti-Communist alliances, and leaving developing countries, driven to "wars of liberation," as easy targets for Communist propaganda.

Instead of military alliances to contain Communism there would be trade and marketing alliances with the emphasis upon pooling resources in the interest of scientific advance, sharing technical assistance, and development of world community. The developing nations would be encouraged and supported in their revolutionary aspirations and in their determination to achieve economic, political and social progress.

There are great areas of the world, including some of the "Capitalist" countries of the West, in which the belief is widespread that Communist methods of industrial and political organization are more effective in raising the levels of life in the developing countries and carrying them toward the point of economic take-off than are the economic and political processes of Western society. Communism is feared and fought by the West not only because of its characteristic evils but because successes in such fields as economic development, education, and welfare in the Soviet Union and in China raise doubts as to the ability of the Western system to keep pace in meeting the deeply felt needs of the world's poor. Thus deterioration of morale occurs before the real issues are joined. Civilian defense would require that reliance be placed on the inherent strength of the country, the viability of its economic system, and the stability of its political system. The key to strength would be reform rather than military control and discipline. The test of power would be in the capacity of a country to enter the world's market with its ideas, its methods, and its products, and demonstrate ability not only in terms of survival but also in willingness to change, to improve, and to grow. The Western political and economic system has shown great flexibility and power during the last half century. Despite unresolved problems of poverty in the midst of plenty, over very significant areas the standards of life have been raised, the opportunities for effective participation in government have been extended, and the capacities for technological advance have risen in a truly spectacular manner. Foreign policy based on civilian defense would mean that these Western capacities could be put to the test of competitive coexistence with the Communist forms of organization and power. If freedom is characteristic of Western society and if it is as firmly the source of social power as our society has claimed, there should be no fear of this competition.

The goals of such policies would still be set at many points in terms of the East-West encounter, but the encounter would be transformed by the readiness of Western civilian defense countries to:

1. Help Communist countries reach the point of economic growth and development where they would be forced by internal pressures to relax domestic controls, and where they would be persuaded by their own economic and social accomplishments to permit a more open society.

2. Hold out to Communist countries the prospect of greater benefits through peaceful co-existence than they can expect through cold war hostility or hot war military assault.

3. Help friendly and nonaligned developing countries to achieve their social and political revolution by peaceful change and development, and to offer them a dynamic alternative to acceptance of Communist control.

4. Encourage other nations, both Communist and non-Communist, to join in the economic and political development of the world community of nations, including civilian

defense of each by all the others in case of military aggression.

THE PURSUIT OF THE CIVILIAN DEFENSE FOREIGN POLICY GOALS

Each of these major foreign policy goals should have its own distinctive perspective and emphasis. In nearly every case policy perspectives would not be entirely different from the perspectives of a military-based policy but the emphasis would be entirely different so that the situation would be largely transformed.

In dealing with Communist countries the United States, relying upon civilian defense, would identify and support the legitimate goals of growth and development, scientific development, and security in the community of nations. In a sense there is nothing revolutionary about such a policy. The United States has, over a period of years, moved from a strict policy of isolation, hostility, and exclusion with respect to the Soviet Union to a policy which embraces nearly every phase of the policy suggested here. Despite earlier fears of Soviet success we have come to see that the attainment by the Soviet Union of the legitimate goals listed above has resulted in less tension, less hostility, and greater opportunities for the development of confidence, trust and genuine security relations than had existed before. As education has risen in the Soviet Union the people have gained confidence, have moved out across the world, have become acquainted with the peoples and the conditions in other lands, and have realized their own capacity for constructive accomplishment. This has led to cultural and scientific exchange, to a more varied participation in the intellectual and political life of the world community, and to an appreciation of the complexity of life in the modern world which cannot be entirely explained in terms of any single dogma or ideology.

Even so, the United States still honors to some extent the

myth that it is desirable to thwart the Soviet Union's efforts toward economic improvement. United States policy toward China is structured entirely along these lines, both in theory and in practice. This adherence to a dogma of ideological antagonism, despite the experience we have had with its self-defeating aspects, is anchored in commitments to military defense. Once these commitment have been discarded it will become both possible and necessary to affirm the right of any country or people to choose the form of government it wishes. Communism's record of coming to power undemocratically, through takeover by a minority, raises problems in this regard. We believe that this must be solved not by United States opposition to self-determination, which is equally undemocratic, but through internationally supervised elections and the maintenance of civil liberties by means including nonviolent struggle.

In dealing with friendly or nonaligned developing countries, the United States would encourage them to exercise power and responsibility in the United Nations. The major problem in the achievement of world community lies in the fact that the United Nations has not yet clearly gained the capacity to maintain its authority as the representative of world opinion in the face of the clear resistance of the United States or the Soviet Union, particularly in the case of the United States. The predominant influence of any super-power in a world body raises questions as to whether the world body is expressive of corporate opinion rather than a façade for the foreign policy of a particular nation. Corporate opinion cannot be expressed in a vacuum, but the rise in influence within the United Nations of the new nations, which can scarcely aspire to super-status, but which together can carry the United Nations in the direction of a genuine parliament of man could undergird the security of every nation choosing civilian defense as a basis of its policies. Such nations would, in effect, place their security in the keeping of the United Nations even as they developed their own internal capacities for civilian defense resistance to external aggression and invasion.

As an aspect of its desire for a stronger role for the United Nations, the United States, as a phase of its civilian defense policy, would encourage the channelling of economic and technical assistance through international agencies which would be controlled in large part by the recipient nations and would operate within a context politically protected from undue influence at the hands of aid-giving nations. In the process of extending aid every effort would be made to downgrade the importance of a nation's political and economic system.

It must be acknowledged that a new nation, moving into the community of nations in the modern world after a century or more of colonial control and exploitation, faces problems of development and utilization of resources which may require discipline and concentration of energies not useful after the initial period of capital accumulation. At this time aid skillfully extended and used can greatly ease the difficulties, but there is no magic formula. There will be many instances where one form or another of dictatorial control will be resorted to during this period. Often it will seem unavoidable if not necessary. A civilian defense aid-extending country will understand such tendencies, even if it does not approve of them, and will help such countries to move on to the point where internal aspirations and pressures and national accomplishments will make relaxation of control both possible and necessary. The critical question will not be whether pure democracy is observed at every step but whether the course followed is one which moves toward security based on community, government based on consent and participation, and life based on respect and opportunity. It should not be too difficult to determine whether a given government is basing its legitimacy and its use of power on the needs and aspirations of the people, or on the preservation of the privileges which formerly were the prerogatives of the few.

It is sad but true that there are elements of human exploitation in almost any period of capital accumulation. Aid which is administered by an international agency, clearly not linked to military intervention or pressure, which makes use of the resources of modern technology to meet the needs of the people in developing countries, could go far to reduce the degree of human exploitation.

If countries basing their policies on civilian defense committed themselves to using their capacities, not to accumulate weapons, but to meet human need, it is possible that they could solve the problem of how to help carry a developing country out of its depressed conditions into full participation in the community of modern nations. This is the point of greatest vulnerability the Western nations face as they confront the Communist claim that they can more effectively solve the problems of economic development of the new nations. Despite vast quantities of aid extended during the two decades following World War II, this problem has not been and cannot be solved within the cold war context. Policies of civilian defense, however, would release vast resources now committed to arms, and would lay the basis for political relationships which make possible genuine development and national fulfillment.

In dealing with other countries possessing an advanced technology the United States, having committed itself to civilian defense, would pool its resources under United Nations supervision for the extension of aid, the development of trade among the nations, and the provision of security support. It would seek to identify goals which would be of benefit to the entire world community, or to a number of nations, and which could not be achieved by any of them separately. Such projects as the development of the Mekong River in the Indo-Chinese peninsula would become major objectives of foreign policy, and primary means of drawing numbers of nations, both Communist and non-Communist nations in efforts of mutual benefit which could not be carried forward unless the developed nations were willing to bring their technical expertise to the service of the international community. The new nations would have to sufficiently submerge their rivalries and sensitivities to questions of status to permit the project to move forward.

A number of our present allies would probably take up a civilian defense policy of their own; indeed, some of them would probably adopt such a policy before the United States. Realistically, it is unlikely that a significant movement for civilian defense could develop in any one country without similar movements developing in comparable industrialized and socially literate countries. Such movements do not necessarily grow into political significance simply as the result of a charismatic personality or effective propaganda but out of a world-wide emergency such as is posed today by the threat of nuclear war.

Moreover, a civilian defense policy would enable nations to accomplish far more than they would under a policy based on military means. They would be free to take initiatives based on their own understandings. Their economies would no longer be burdened by the enormous demands of the military, yet they would not feel oppressed by dependence on the United States for security, since their reliance would be on the developing world community and on their own civilian defense system.

CIVIL ALLIANCES

It might be found useful to set up "civil alliances" composed of nations which have adopted civilian defense systems and have pledged to come to each other's aid if attacked. In addition to economic sanctions and political pressure, the governments might choose to send in cadres of nonviolent forces.

If unilateral disarmament by the United States did not lead quickly to world-wide disarmament and a basic transformation of the United Nations into an effective world authority, the United States could take the lead in forming a subsidiary group analogous to the regional organizations provided for in the United Nations Charter. The United States would invite all nations that disarmed to join in a new alliance for mutual assistance in the promotion of international peace. If any member of the new alliance were to be menaced by an armed aggressor, the member nations would mobilize their political and economic resources in a peace offensive to forestall outright invasion or to render military blackmail ineffective or inoperative.

Before the advent of either unilateral disarmament or international alliances citizen groups could take the lead in forging instruments for international nonviolent action, including peace-keeping functions. In today's world, it is quite conceivable that a nation—one of the nations in Africa, for example— might call upon international volunteers trained in nonviolent action, rather than get caught up in a catastrophic military operation at or within its borders.

The success of such enterprises—if that be their fortune— could impart momentum to the growth of nonviolence in the political field, develop experience and confidence in tests of power based on nonviolent action, and at the same time provide additional security arrangements for the nation committed to the hard tasks of the interim period prior to world-wide disarmament. It could be the beginning of a world community which would make questions of national sovereignty relatively less important. It would enhance the sense of the mind, purpuse, and authority of the world community. In addition to actual constitutional authority, it would eventually bring into reality the disestablishment of war as a part of the international system.

THE REALIZATION OF THE GOALS OF
CIVILIAN DEFENSE FOREIGN POLICY

The long range goal of civilian defense is a world in which it would be inconceivable that one nation would war against another. Although today we are far from this goal, we can see the embryonic growth of security communities. The Am-

erican Friends Service Comittee report, *A New China Policy,*
states it this way:

> The great object before us from which we should never be
> deterred is the achievement of a world security community—
> a world in which 'each shall live under his own vine and his
> own fig tree and none shall make them afraid;' a world in
> which threats and counterthreats no longer rule the relations
> of men and nations. A security community is not an idle
> dream; over sections of the world it already exists. In Scandi-
> navia, among the English-speaking countries, recently in
> Western Europe, and among the socialist states, groups of
> nations have emerged within which war becomes increasingly
> improbable; war is no longer a factor in the behavior of these
> nations toward one another.[1]

The ultimate achievement of a world community does not depend upon any particular formal international structure,
though this may eventually emerge. Of far greater importance
is the establishment of systems available to the international
community for the settlement of conflict without resort to
military measures—systems which will exist according to acknowledged principles based on the rights and dignity of every
nation.

The achievement of such a world community may be a long
way off. We must assume that there may still be a period of
wars and invasions, which must be absorbed and repelled by
civilian defense. They can also be made useless and senseless
because of the security and advantage available to every nation through the processes and the relationships of peaceful
co-existence and the development of the world community.

The fact that war is irrational does not keep it from happen-
ing. Most wars have been irrational. Even so, the recognition
of the irrationality of war, if it is firmly and repeatedly demon-
strated, and if nations as a matter of declared policy and
practice begin to turn from its preparations and its policies,

[1](New Haven: Yale University Press, 1965).

can at least provide the grounds for removing war as an aspect of the international system.

A STUDY IN CONTRASTS

Even a relatively successful foreign policy based on military defense is often in certain crucial aspects self-defeating; one based on civilian defense would be self-fulfilling. It is to the advantage of the non-Communist countries to see the Communist countries develop along lines of individuality, yet the influence of their military policies is to drive the Communist countries into alliances which otherwise could not be sustained. Civilian defense would stimulate them to develop according to their somewhat separate needs and tendencies and allow the emergence of freer societies. They could accept aid without feeling threatened and it would be given to them for purposes of building a security community rather than for a program of military defense.

It is to the advantage of the developed nations to see new governments and systems emerge to replace old tyrannies. Military necessity all too often has dictated the establishment of alliances with corrupt governments propping up old tyranny. Civilian defense would be based on aid to new governments laying new foundations for freedom and development in which there would be no need for nor advantage in military aggression.

It is in the interest of the United States to see our allies confident in our reliability as a friend in time of need. Military alliances create apprehension in times of crisis because the hazards of fulfilling military commitments in the nuclear age are very high. A policy based on the encouragement of world community in the context of civilian defense would stake vital interests on the security of every segment of that community; fulfillment of commitments would become a matter of self-interest.

In this connection it is not difficult to see the emergence of a new kind of international force arising out of the accumulated experience of private and public programs of international aid and assistance such as the Peace Corps. Throughout the early years of violent civil war in South Vietnam educational, agricultural, and health workers of the International Voluntary Service worked unarmed and unmolested in many parts of the country, some controlled by Saigon and some by the National Liberation Front. If such civilian volunteers can be a stabilizing and a constructive element even in the midst of war, how much greater would be the opportunity if one or both sides based foreign policy on such activities and invited men of good will from many countries to come and carry forward the necessary works of peace.

WOULD IT WORK?

Would a foreign policy based on civilian defense work? Would it carry the world out of the morass of policies based on military defense, which now only increases the instability? We do not know. What we do know is that human society has at last reached a stage of development in which the very capacities and demands which have been created by what has gone before—by the achievements of man—confront all mankind with basic challenges which can only be met if wars cease.

We are now at the end of an era in which strength and power generated by war, by the skillful use of economic scarcity, and by the limitation of the franchise have led the world into an impasse and to the brink of disaster. If we are to survive and move forward, we must learn to rely on peace, accept abundance, and heed the voice of the powerless. Those who live by the sword will now be destroyed by it, for weapons can no longer be managed and used rationally. Those who have grown rich and powerful by manipulating scarcity are about to be overwhelmed by abundance. And those who have been denied a voice and a place are now shaking the foundations of government and must be heard. There is change in the basic situation. Nations must at last abandon military establishments for the sake of survival; economic systems must accept the principle of abundance and fulfill its potential or else go under; governments must express the mind of the forgotten and the excluded or lose the capacity to govern. Whether governments based on nonviolent sanctions can survive, whether economies of abundance can flourish, or whether a truly universal franchise is possible remains to be seen. But these are the inexorable demands which history now places upon mankind as a condition of survival.

5 | What Do We Do Now?

The American people have combined practicality with a willingness to venture into the wil·lerness. That is how the country got started. The time has come again to leave the old familiar ways and risk the unexplored continent for the sake of the new home we can build there—in the community of a world without war. We believe that civilian defense can succeed. But today only the outlines of such a policy exists. It is important to consider, therefore, what we can do right now to move our nation closer to the day when a nonviolent defense policy will exist.

In our scenario the United States considered such a policy only after a nuclear weapon had been smuggled onto its soil and one of its major cities had been destroyed by an unexplainable nuclear explosion. This scenario may seem fanciful at points, but there is nothing fanciful about the situation in which the explosion and the smuggling occurred. We are already well advanced toward the time when, unless there is a drastic change in policy, such things could happen. If such events were to occur, the President and his advisers would doubtless re-examine our nuclear policies. We call on the nation to support such re-examination *now* without waiting to be convinced by nuclear disaster.

Though a total training program such as we have outlined cannot be launched without a national decision to do so, some things can and must be done *now* to win support for civilian defense. Those who are willing to work to spread the idea of civilian defense should become competent critics of nuclear deterrence, informed about foreign policy issues, adept at encouraging discussion and practical projects, familiar with the great struggles in which nonviolence has played a role. They should be participants in current constructive change in our social order; they should be involved in nonviolent protest action against war and militarism, aware of the special conditions which must be met if civilian defense is to become national policy; they should be pioneers in efforts to provide materials and methods for training in nonviolence. Studies such as these can be useful tools. People are needed who will work in their own communities, speaking, explaining, encouraging, suggesting, as opportunities arise. There is even greater need for people to analyze how civilian defense would operate in their own real-life situations, and how preparations would be made in the institutions which will exert social control in case of attack or invasion.

Each of the basic institutions of society has made its own accommodation to the nuclear deterrence situation; each needs now to find its creative role in civilian defense in the light of alternative strategies and various types of threats. For such institutions discussion and analysis of resources which they can bring to civilian defense might develop along the following lines:

1. *The Military*

Members of the military establishment will need to re-examine their roles in light of the inadequacy of present defense policies and the potentials of civilian defense. The problem of replacing military power with nonviolent power in international conflict is central to this entire study. The following changes must occur if nonviolent means are to be used in dealing with international conflict.

a. Nonviolent action must be transformed from a minority expression of social protest into a majority expression of national will.

b. Specific training programs in nonviolent methods of national defense must be organized by the government.

c. Nonviolent defense measures must be developed with the same energy and thoroughness that now characterize military defense measures.

Although it is not easy for military men to think in terms of civilian defense, it is certainly not impossible, for national defense is their responsibility. The military are increasingly aware that armed conflict is fraught with colossal pitfalls and they do not all romanticize the nuclear bomb. Civilian defense can furnish them with a constructive way in which to fulfill their responsibility to defend the country.

It is a very hopeful sign that military officers and theorists have already given some consideration to the possibilities of civilian defense. Though it is still on a small scale, research in nonviolent techniques is now being carried on within the Pentagon and by quasi-governmental research organizations. Little information is available about this research. In fact, one gets the impression that the aim is to prepare to counter the use of nonviolent methods by opponents, rather than to anticipate that the United States might someday employ them. Even so the training and capacity of military men will be needed to deal with questions of strategy and tactics in the development of civilian defense. For this research to bear fruit, increased appropriations for further research and development are greatly needed.

The role of the military in preparing the United States for civilian defense can hardly be overemphasized. Other social institutions can help pave the way, but unless the military considers these proposals seriously and develops them, the likelihood of the United States adopting civilian defense is slight. As we have pointed out, civilian defense must be initiated by the government with the support—or at least the consent—of the people. It is possible that the "military-industrial elite" could block civilian defense. Certainly a civilian defense policy would diminish the power of this enormously powerful part of our society. On the other hand, the growth of confidence which a world at peace would provide for every segment of society would more than compensate for losses of special influence and prestige.

2. The Universities

The universities offer the intellectual base for change. Here we note a new readiness to re-exmine the old premises. Although since World War II the universities have increasingly become the servant of the military-industrial complex—and indeed have done much of the weapons research—they have also begun creative exploration into the possibility of a nonviolent ordering in international affairs. Members of university faculties and student bodies have played leading roles in questioning policies and protesting commitments to military solutions for social and economic problems.

Continued and extended exploration needs to be encouraged. How can the power of nonviolent action be related to the realities of international affairs, to the end that the power relationships between states can find expression in other than military terms? What institutions need to be built to express these kinds of power? What training programs are required to prepare men to use them? How can they be utilized in particular situations? Answers to these and other questions must be sought. The university has a role to play.

3. *The Churches and Religious Bodies.*

That religious faith can help create the structures of world community and remove war from the earth is suggested by the response evoked by Pope John XXIII's encyclical, *Pacem in Terris;* that religious resources can erect the defenses of non-violent action is suggested with equal conviction by the new power evidenced in the life of the churches as they have moved courageously into the civil rights struggle in the United States.

Instead of using religion as a means of justifying accommodations to the "lesser evil" of increasingly ruthless and savage war, civilian defense would find in religion resources for realizing love and justice through nonviolence. There are indeed tremendous spiritual resources which the churches and synagogues can release if they preach, teach, and practice nonviolence as a source of power for the nations, following the example of Jeremiah, of Isaiah, of St. Francis of Assisi, and of Gandhi.

A national policy of civilian defense would open the way for the religious bodies to do just this, just as the Supreme Court decision of 1954 gave great new impetus to the churches of the United States to oppose segregation and racial discrimination. But why wait for national policy to open the way for the churches to act for peace? We believe that the churches should be in the vanguard, challenging leaders and common citizens alike to reject nuclear war and pursue a radically new and different policy of national defense.

4. *Business and Industry*

Many of the skills and methods developed to increase armaments production are now required to meet human needs throughout the world. However, the demand for weapons, on the one hand, and doubt about U. S. motives (inevitable in the present cold war frame of reference), on the other hand, severely limit the nation's ability to meet such needs. Under civilian defense American industry, freed of those limiting factors, could help to meet the problems of human need both at home and abroad. Industrial organizations could embark upon research and the development of both products and methods to solve the problems of human need. The vast resources of the government which have been used to finance contracts with industry for the development and production of weaponry could be diverted to the financing of contracts for new civilian purposes. Civilian defense need not be accompanied by an economic collapse due to the wholesale cancellation of government contracts. Federal spending is essential to enable private industry to find solutions to the problems of health, communications, transportation, housing, and education, which have long been neglected by the commitment of federal resources to the arms race and the cold war.

Today, particularly in defense industry, industrialists have mastered the technique of tackling large and complicated production problems by using a "systems" approach. Many of these efforts are financed through government contracts with private industry, utilizing the resources of a wide variety of research establishments to devise and produce weapons systems and to develop war plans. There is no reason that this same basic approach could not be directed toward the solution of problems of human need.

In the absence of a decision by the United States to adopt civilian defense as a basic policy, businessmen and industrialists, with government encouragement and financial aid, can begin the study and analysis of how modern productive capacities can be fully utilized for peaceful purposes, since this is a problem which must be faced regardless of the nature of our foreign policy. As we gain confidence in our capacity to use our productive resources for human ends, we create within society the elements of a system of civilian defense.

5. *The Trade Unions*

The unions are becoming aware that their accommodation to the arms race is not an unmixed blessing. Despite the enormous government contracts, arms production is not a reliable stimulus to jobs and full employment. Unions have an important stake in recasting industry to provide more employment to meet human need and to reduce labor's reliance on military contracts. In their struggle to organize and survive, the unions learned many methods of nonviolent action, such as strikes and boycotts. Experienced unionists know the art of organization and of maintaining morale under pressure when each day is filled with danger and uncharted hazards. The unions have survived because they have been led by people who could move from hostile conflict in the streets directly to the bargaining table where accommodations had to be made in terms of the immediate realities. All this involves skills essential to civilian defense.

As an initial step now, leading unions should appoint Peace Planning Directors to their educational and research staffs to do the following:

a. Relate the problems of cybernation in the context of nuclear deterrence to the opportunities of conversion of a peace-time economy;

b. Stimulate thought and discussion among the membership about civilian defense as an alternative to nuclear war.

6. *The Peace Movement*

Since civilian defense must be accepted by the government and the people in advance of a crisis, many civilian defense theorists believe that such proposals can best be initiated and developed as a matter of practical necessity by strategic specialists or by the government itself. They believe that peace actionists do a disservice to civilian defense proposals by confusing them with religiously based pacifist approaches. One purpose of this inquiry is to reduce confusion in this area.

We do not wish to discount the great contributions which morally-based nonviolent direct action for peace can make to the acceptance of civilian defense. In fact, we believe it possible that this approach might be more effective in the long run than the traditional approaches of research and education, though the two are certainly not mutually exclusive.

Gandhi advocated the creation of "parallel institutions" which could take over the power of established institutions when they proved unworkable. The World Peace Brigade[1] was an early attempt to provide a nonviolent parallel institution for the resolution of international conflict. It was premature and died. Perhaps in the future it will be revived or a comparable effort will be initiated which will be more successful.

Let us assume, for example, the creation of an international Peace Brigade of ten thousand persons trained in nonviolent techniques and willing to face the hazards of a war situation. Let us suppose that such a brigade could be landed in South Vietnam to march on military headquarters in Saigon with the following demands: (1) an immediate cease-fire; (2) the immediate withdrawal of U. S. and other foreign troops; (3) the demilitarization of Southeast Asia under the supervision of the nations that participated in the Geneva Conference in 1954; (4) internationally supervised elections in South Vietnam and eventual reunification with North Vietnam. Would such an approach be workable? Would it provide a pattern for the introduction of nonviolent methods into other war situations?

For the time being, these questions will remain academic. The suggested project far exceeds the resources of the present nonviolent peace movement. Yet, the possibility of the eventual development of nonviolent parallel institutions relevant to international conflict should not be discounted.

7.   *The Civil Rights Movement*

Although, as we have pointed out earlier, the nonviolent

---

[1]Founded in 1962. Sponsored a training school in Tanganyika and the Delhi-Peking Walk.

methods used by the civil rights movement will not necessarily or automatically lead to civilian defense as a national policy, the experiences of nonviolent resistance and struggle which have carried the civil rights movement forward constitute a tremendous source of confidence and strength for the advocates of civilian defense. The adoption of civilian defense requires a national decision which the leadership of the civil rights movement can help to create.

Significant civil rights leadership is aware of the nuclear context in which it is operating. The awareness will deepen as problems of securing employment become more and more understood in terms of an armaments weighted economy, as opportunities for genuine social participation are seen in the context of a world without war, and as the parallels between the civil rights problems at home and the problems of the new nations abroad are more fully understood.

Concern over Vietnam has drawn many who have been involved in the civil rights movement into broad participation in the anti-war movement, and suggests the possibility of their support for civilian defense. Questions to be considered might include the following:

a. In what ways would resisting an invader be similar to and different from resisting racism in Alabama or Mississippi?
b. Under such circumstances, what can be expected of the ordinary person? What is too much to expect?
c. How much and what kind of training ahead of time is helpful?
d. Is it realistic to think of the civil rights movement becoming a strong component of a civilian defense movement?

Other equally pertinent questions would arise, and additional areas to be examined would emerge from such a discussion.

The civil rights movement can become the single most important factor in civilian defense. Though the aims of the Negroes are not revolutionary in themselves they *are* revolutionary in that they can be achieved only by radical new approaches to the job problem, the education problem, and the housing problem in the United States. The civil rights movement, by insisting that these problems can be solved and by basing its insistence on nonviolence, simultaneously shakes the foundations of the status quo and *proves that nonviolent action is a source of power. What still is needed is to relate that source of power to the problem of international conflict.* To this task Martin Luther King, the civil rights leader, called us in his speech of acceptance of the 1964 Nobel Peace Price, as he said:

> Nonviolence is the answer to the crucial political and moral question of our time—the need for man to overcome oppressions and violence without resorting to violence and oppression . . . .
>
> Negroes of the United States, following the people of India, have demonstrated that nonviolence is not sterile passivity, but a powerful moral force which makes for social transformation. Sooner or later all the people of the world will have to discover a way to live together in peace, and thereby transform this pending cosmic elegy into a creative psalm of brotherhood.
>
> If this is to be achieved, man must evolve for all human conflict a method which rejects revenge, aggression and retaliation. The foundation of such a method is love.

*The New York Times, December 11, 1964.

CONCLUSION

We must begin now to prepare for and even to initiate the changes that will be required if our country is someday to adopt a civilian defense policy. If such a policy is to succeed, there must be positive movement now in all institutions within our society not toward Utopia, but rather toward a dynamic, forward-looking and forward-moving society in the development of which all our citizens may share, and in the success of which all our people may have a vital interest. In such a society, in times of serenity as well as in times of stress, people will be conscious of their identification with others. Farmer and laborer, Negro and white, city dweller and suburbanite, Jew and Gentile, northerner and southerner—each will be conscious of working together in time of peace and of standing fast together in times of conflict.

Assuredly, if what we envisage as essential for the security of each of the basic institutions that has made its own accommodation to nuclear deterrence prepare now for a reorientation of national policy. No institution dare wait until the nation has decided upon a policy of civilian defense, but every institution instead should constitute an influence moving the country in that direction.

Assuredly, if what we evisage as essential for the security of both the world community and the nation is ever to be realized tomorrow, we must start today to think, study, search, plan, imagine, experiment, hope, work and generally move in that direction.

6 | The
Calculated Risk

As we review our work on this document, we recall a dilemma that has plagued us throughout. We have continuously divided as to how we deal with the relation between the truly revolutionary and salutary results that might follow the implementation of civilian defense and the possibility that a militarily disarmed United States might instead be attacked and invaded.

UNLIKELIHOOD OF INVASION

It is our considered judgment that, if the changes we have suggested were made in United States foreign policy, a physical invasion of our nation would be highly unlikely. Certainly no power acting with any slight degree of rationality would attempt it. Why?

Our answer falls into three parts.

1. What would another nation have to gain by invading a United States which had adopted policies of civilian defense and moved far along the lines suggested above? Any nation wishing to benefit economically would achieve far more by trading with America than by invading; the costs and uncertainty of an invasion would be enormous compared to those of trade. Civilians commonly underestimate the difficulties of launching a large-scale invasion, especially with the training of men and massing of material and transport that would be involved.

It is also difficult to see what political gains could be achieved through invading the United States committed to civilian defense. Neither the Soviet Union nor China would fear military invasion from this country—any more than today they fear military invasion from New Zealand or from Zambia. Our absence of military preparations would contribute to their sense of security, providing every inducement for them to respond, not by military invasion, but rather by competitive disarmament and nonmilitary (including cultural and commercial) competition.

From the standpoint of economic potential, the United States would be at a tremendous advantage, devoting its full energies to trade and economic aid. To continue its political influence in the world an opponent would be compelled to follow in the direction of the United States, thus minimizing the danger of invasion still more.

2. An important factor in past invasions, especially in creating the necessary support to mount and sustain them, has been found in ideological considerations. The invasion appeared necessary to preserve or advance a national ideology. Here again, if we identify the Communist world as our potential enemy, the ideological factor would be minimized in the situation under discussion. A United States with a civilian defense policy would so completely belie Marxist teaching about the nature of the American social system, its inherent dependence upon violence, and its aggressive and exploitative

character that it would be extremely difficult to muster support inside—and certainly outside—the Communist world for a costly invasion of the United States.

3. Finally, let us note certain military impediments to a possible invasion. George F. Kennan suggested in his Reith Lectures of 1957 that even if the West had not formed NATO in 1949, the Soviet Union would probably not have invaded Western Europe. Its lines of communications would have been over-extended; it would have been confronted by the overwhelming opposition of highly developed populations such as those of France and Italy; and controlling its own troops in the presence of much higher standards of living would have become virtually impossible. If this were so of Western Europe, how much more would it apply to controlling a non-violently defended United States, not only opposed to the invader, but equipped with a carefully developed system of nonviolent non-cooperation to implement that opposition? A similiar but stronger observation could be made about Mainland China.

The logistical and manpower requirements are also such formidable impediments to invasion that a militarily disarmed United States would scarcely be faced or threatened by invasion. During the occupation of Norway in World War II, for example, the Germans were forced to commit troops in the ratio of about one German to ten Norwegians, even though widespread open resistance did not exist. In other words, it required between 250,000 and 400,000 German troops to control 3,500,000 Norwegians. Comparable figures for the United States would suggest an invasion force of at least 20,000,000 men! How would such an army be transported across wide oceans? How would supply and communications lines be maintained over thousands of miles? How would an enemy nation handle the domestic problems created by such a vast invasion enterprise? Moreover, since world standards of living would inevitably make a devastating impact on occupying troops, rotation would be essential. How would this be managed? What would be the impact of millions of dissatisfied troops returning to the enemy population?

In the light of such considerations, the adoption of a policy of civilian defense by the United States would apparently go a long way toward making invasion of our shores both unreasonable and improbable. The critic may, of course, suggest that there are risks in developing a nonviolent defense policy along the lines we have suggested. This we readily admit; breaking with the past always involves risks and uncertainties. One of these risks lies in the unlikely possibility that we might, in spite of all reason to the contrary, be invaded.

Such an eventually must be faced frankly. Therefore, although all of us in the working party unite in believing that invasion would be unlikely if a great power like the United States broke the stalemate by introducing a radically new civilian defense element into the world situation, we have deliberately de-emphasized the probable socio-psychological effects of the advocated change. Let us assume that an armed invasion might follow, an invasion that would go to considerable lengths in its efforts to conquer us and suppress all opposition, but we will *not* assume that the invaders would carry out the systematic and total destruction of our nation.

IF CONFRONTED BY POSSIBLE ANNIHILATION

Annihilation is also a possibility, albeit remote. A nation might exist that is so immoral and ruthless it would immolate even an obviously peaceful and friendly country. And—the world might simply stand by and let this happen. However, those who insist that we must posit such an assumption and base national policy on it, cannot leave the matter there. If as a matter of fact, we have to deal with a nation or nations so devoid both of reason and of moral decency as to be capable of destroying an unarmed and friendly people, then we are lost in any event. Such a nation by hypothesis would be powerfully armed. If it were not, its threat would not have to be taken seriously. In today's world a heavily armed nation devoid of all rationality and decency may in the end force a nuclear showdown on us and the rest of mankind. In these circumstances, deterrence would break down.

If that moment of ultimate terror arrives, we shall have only two possible courses of action before us. One will be to resort to the use of the weapons which we had amassed precisely to "deter the enemy" and avoid such a moment. We would thereby join in the senseless slaughter, becoming co-perpetrators of the murder of civilization and perhaps the extinction of the race. The other possibility would be to draw back from so insane an act and to accept the risk of being slaughtered.

Faced with these stark alternatives, we feel warranted in turning back to a position stated a few years ago by George F. Kennan in an address to the students of Princeton Theological Seminary. He proposed that the United States never again resort to the use of nuclear or other weapons of mass destruction, thus making "the men, women, and children of another nation the hostages for the behavior of their government."[1] He suggested that if we should be attacked we should defend our homes by such direct means as might be available, but should in no case resort to mass slaughter.

To the suggestion that this would mean national defeat Kennan replied that he did not know what defeat was, or victory, in modern war waged with mass destruction weapons. In any event, he went on, there are moments when people should trust in God, and in that measure of reason and decency which even their enemies possess.

If Kennan is right in his assumption that in even the most implacable enemy there is a minimum of decency and some

---

[1] A lecture, "Certain World Problems in the Christian Perspective," delivered on January 27, 1959 as one of "The Challenge to the Church Series" of lectures given at Princeton Theological Seminary.
NOTE: A book of selected papers prepared for the Civilian Defense Study Conference, held at Oxford University (England) September, 1964, will soon be published, along with new material, by Faber (London), Adam Roberts, Editor.

realization of our common human predicament, then hope replaces despair. If there are some such elements even in those whose present behavior is or appears to be inordinately cruel and oppressive, it behooves us to place reliance in a national policy that will appeal mightily to such elements both among those whom we number as our enemies, and among all the members of the family of men. To us this is realism. A policy of civilian defense takes decency into account. It is predicated upon the belief that in the final analysis the vast majority of men throughout the world will respond positively and affirmatively to the sort of friendly and constructive approach that we have outlined in earlier chapters.

Were we actually to put this approach into active practice in a nonviolent foreign and defense policy for the United States, we might find that other nations would follow our example, even other groups of nations. Then, instead of stumbling down the blind alley of nuclear destruction with our fellow men, we would demonstrate before the world our reliance upon other methods for our defense and chart a course which others might follow with hope.

We have dealt only slightly with the United States' responsibility to former military allies after adopting civilian defense. Invasion or take-over of these nations would be far more probable than an all-out invasion of a civilian defense-armed United States. But let us point out that the allies of the United States face these problems today, in spite of our vast military might. In fact, we would venture to suggest that even without civilian defense the United States could develop nonmilitary approaches to the problems of Southeast Asia, Africa, and Latin America that would provide security far more effectively than the military means now employed. Present means, as we have pointed out, tend to ally the United States with undemocratic reactionary elements in these countries. Such elements are bound to be repudiated in the long run, regardless of American military might. President Johnson confirms that our ultimate aim in Vietnam is to win the hearts and minds of men.

We believe that the United States could accomplish this far more effectively through civilian defense than with the largest armies and all the weapons in the world.

We don't mean to suggest easy answers to these problems; they are enormously complex. No one need warn us that there are tremendous risks involved in civilian defense. That we know full well. But these risks are less than those of nuclear deterrence. We believe that the people of the world would respond with unparalleled expressions of gratitude and joy to civilian defense leadership by the United States.

This would be the nation of which Ralph Waldo Emerson spoke in 1838, a nation of men who had broken with war because "they have not so much madness left in their brains." He characterized it as a nation "which has a friend in the bottom of the heart of every man, even the violent and the base; one against which no weapons can prosper; and which is looked upon as the asylum of the human race and has the tears and blessings of mankind."

Scenario, Part Two

"A dozen years ago my illustrious predecessor, John F. Kennedy, made a much quoted statement, 'Ask not what your country can do for you but what you can do for your country.' Various interpretations have been given, but until today the question of what you can do for your country has really gone unanswered. Today I can tell you quite specifically things you might be called on to do for your country, for today I am proposing that the United States develop a national system of civilian defense based on nonviolence."

Thus spoke the President to the people of America via television six months after the Denver tragedy. He was appearing before a joint session of Congress. Seated behind him were members of his Cabinet and other leaders who would join him in the proposal for nonviolent national defense.

There had been no further explosions. No more smuggled

bombs were found. While the Secretary of Defense continued to maintain that the bomb could not have been American, the prevailing opinion within government circles was that the publicly announced explanation of an accidental detonation was in this case true, even though there were differences of opinion among them as to whether it was a domestic or smuggled bomb.

Senators and Congressmen arose to applaud the President's statement. He looked from face to face as they stood there applauding. In the months previous he had spoken privately with each of them, paving the way for today. It had not been easy. Of the hundreds of leaders he had had to convince, the industrialists and the militarists—that complex Eisenhower had warned about—had been the key group. After they began to line up, the Congress had been less difficult.

The President neared the end of the speech. "Civilian national defense asks nothing new of us in principle, but in practice it demands great changes. In undertaking nonviolent defense we, the American people, will face new risks. I believe I have stated these risks forthrightly. In conclusion let me say that I believe these risks to be far less than the risks we faced for years under our outmoded defense system. These risks of nonviolent national defense are in keeping with the American temper and tradition. They are risks that our courage and our beliefs equip us to meet. In fact, these risks are essential to the preservation of peace and freedom." (Applause.)

"My predecessor spoke of a national consensus when there was no consensus. If this country is to adopt nonviolent national defense, the basis must be a genuine consensus. Today we will introduce legislation establishing a national referendum on civilian defense to take place in one month. By the grace of God and the wisdom of the American people, we will at that time begin to create a national defense in keeping with the great American tradition and equal to the demands of the thermonuclear age."

There was another ovation as he sat down.

The Secretary of Defense spoke next, outlining efficient plans for dismantling the present military machine and for building the civilian defense system. Nuclear weapons would be dismantled immediately and all fissionable material registered with an international body. The rest of the Armed Forces would be phased out over a period of five years.

Military men would be re-educated for fruitful participation in civilian life. A Citizens Task Force would be created immediately. As well as providing for national defense, the Citizens Task Force would offer other nations assistance in establishing their own nonviolent defense system. This task force would number only a few thousand men. There would be no general mobilization for civilian defense unless an emergency threatened. The draft, of course, would be abolished. All national service would be voluntary. The Peace Corps would be expanded and its members given extensive training in nonviolent techniques.

The Secretary of the Treasury then explained economic measures to offset the loss due to conversion from war industry. He predicted an era of unprecedented economic health. With large re-education programs and an increased Guaranteed National Income, individual workers would not suffer.

Next the Secretary of State explained how American military alliances would be altered. Secret consultations with allies and other nations had taken place. While the United States would withdraw immediately from direct military participation, military aid to allied countries would be continued for up to five years. Technical assistance in conversion to civilian defense would also be offered. Increased economic aid to all needy nations would be administered by agencies of the United Nations.

The next speaker was an ex-general, the key leader of the extreme right wing. Although the President was still somewhat uncomfortable with this man, he realized that without his active support the chances of building broad acceptance for nonviolent defense were nil. Since the ex-general's "conver-

sion" *the two had worked as a team convincing other leaders,
especially conservatives and militarists. They had great success.
There were no real holdouts thus far, though they were sure
some would appear in the month before the referendum.*

*"Doubtless many of you are astounded to see me here," he
began. "Doubtless some of you thought I'd never get this close
to the reins of power. Doubtless others of you think I am now
a captive of that Communist conspiracy in Washington I've
warned about for so long. Well, I hope not. It's not easy for a
man like me to eat crow—but I don't know how much crow
I'll have to eat. The fact that I am here does not mean that I
am in complete agreement with the administration. Far from
it. I still believe that Communism is a most pernicious form of
totalitarianism. But I believe that the only way to meet its
challenge is nonviolently, in keeping with the American tradition of freedom and respect for the rights of the individual."*

*Other speakers elaborated on various aspects of nonviolent
national defense. Then the President and his party boarded a
fleet of helicopters for a prearranged meeting at United Nations headquarters. This meeting was to be broadcast throughout the world by television communications satellite.*

*By the time they arrived in New York the streets were filled
with hundreds of thousands of people. They sang and cheered
and chanted. The atmosphere was one of joy. The President
and his party received another standing ovation as they entered
the General Assembly. Already the delegates from Zambia
and Sweden had announced their countries' determination to
join the United States in converting to nonviolent national
defense.*

*The President opened his speech stirringly. "Let no man
mistake what we propose. If our plan is accepted by the American people, as we have strong reason to believe it will be, we
propose to do away with our military defense system completely. We will dismantle our nuclear weapons, destroy our
missiles and our Polaris submarines. We will begin to withdraw our bases in other countries. Within five years we will*

dismantle our military system right down to the last armed soldier. Throughout this process we invite complete inspection by any nation or by any international group.

"Let us make clear however, that we are not disarming. We are transarming to civilian defense. We invite all nations to join us in this process. We fervently hope that all of you will urge this to your governments.

"But let us also be absolutely clear that our transarmament is not dependent upon the actions of other nations. At the time the United States adopts nonviolent national defense, we will consider the process irreversible. We will be prepared to meet any threat to our sovereignty without arms.

"Let us also be crystal clear that the basis for our new security will be justice and freedom for all people. As long as any man anywhere in the world is starving we will not be secure. As long as any man anywhere in the world lacks political freedom, we will not be secure. As long as any man anywhere in the world lives in poverty or in ignorance, none of us will be secure.

"We will put our full economic and technological resources at the disposal of the United Nations to eradicate as quickly as possible these inequities which have been throughout history the causes of war. We are fully convinced that this policy is a practical one. With the grace of God it will herald a new era in the history of the world. For the first time—all men— will be enabled to begin to live up to their human potential.

"We are aware that disputes and conflicts will continue to arise. We are aware that would-be tyrants will appear. We are aware that our new defense policy might force the American people to take upon themselves an unimaginable burden of suffering. But, though these obstacles remain, we are convinced that in choosing nonviolent national defense we are choosing the most practical, the most humane road to lead us through the maze of history. We ask all men to walk with us as brothers down this road."

Again there was an ovation, an expression of joy heard around the world.

Selected Bibliography

Bondurant, Joan, THE CONQUEST OF VIOLENCE,
Princeton University Press, 1958.

Boulding, Kenneth, THE MEANING OF THE TWENTIETH CENTURY,
Harper & Row, New York, 1964.

Bristol, James, NONVIOLENCE IN INDIA TODAY,
American Friends Service Committee, Philadelphia, 1963.

Butterfield, Herbert, INTERNATIONAL CONFLICT IN THE TWENTIETH CENTURY,
Harper & Row, New York, 1960. Note chapter "Human Nature and the Dominion of Fear."

Camus, Albert, "Neither Victims nor Executioners,"
Reprinted in Paul Goodman (ed.), SEEDS OF LIBERATION,
George Braziller, New York, 1964.

Deming, Barbara, PRISON NOTES,
Grossman Publishers, New York, 1966.

Fischer, Louis, GANDHI,
Mentor Books, New American Library, New York, 1954. Most of the material is drawn from the author's full biographical book THE LIFE OF MAHATMA GANDHI, Harper, New York, 1950; published in paperbound edition by Collier Books.

Gandhi, M. K., NONVIOLENCE RESISTANCE,
Schocken Books, New York, 1961. Published in India as SATYAGRAHA, Navajivan Trust, Ahmedabad, 1951.

Gregg, Richard B., THE POWER OF NONVIOLENCE,
Fellowship Publications, Nyack, New York, 1959, Second Revised Edition. First Published in 1934 by Lippincott.

Jack, Homer (ed.), THE GANDHI READER,
Indiana University Press, Bloomington, Ind., 1956.

King-Hall, Stephen, DEFENSE IN THE NUCLEAR AGE,
Fellowship Publications, Nyack, New York, 1959.

Kuper, Leo, PASSIVE RESISTANCE IN SOUTH AFRICA,
Yale University Press, New Haven, 1957.

Larson, Arthur (ed.), A WARLESS WORLD,
McGraw-Hill, New York, 1963. Note Appendix which includes a conversation on "The Russian Idea of a World without War."

Lens, Sidney, REVOLUTION AND COLD WAR,
American Friends Service Committee, Philadelphia, 1962. In the Beyond Deterrence Series.

Lyttle, Bradford, NATIONAL DEFENSE THROUGH NONVIOLENT RESISTANCE,
Shahn-ti Sena Publications, Chicago, 1958.

Miller, William Robert,
NONVIOLENCE: A CHRISTIAN INTERPRETATION,
Association Press, New York, 1964.

Millis, Walter, AN END TO ARMS,
Atheneum, New York, 1965.

Muste, A. J., "Politics on the Other Side of Despair," reprinted in Paul Goodman (ed.), SEEDS OF LIBERATION, George Braziller, New York, 1964.

———— , "Tiger at the Gates," reprinted in Paul Goodman (ed.), SEEDS OF LIBERATION, George Braziller, New York, 1964.

Olson, Theodore and Christiansen, Gordon, THIRTY-ONE HOURS, Canadian Friends Service Committee, Toronto, 1966.

Rapoport, Anatol, STRATEGY AND CONSCIENCE, Harper & Row, New York, 1964.

Roberts, Adam (ed.), CIVILIAN DEFENSE, Peace News, London, 1964. Co-authors: Jerome Frank, Arne Naess and Gene Sharp. Forward by Alastair Buchan.

———— , THE STRATEGY OF CIVILIAN DEFENSE, Faber and Faber, London, 1967.

Roberts, Adam and Sharp, Gene (eds.), DEFENSE WITHOUT WAR, Walker & Co., New York, 1967.

Sharp, Gene, THE POLITICAL EQUIVALENT OF WAR— CIVILIAN DEFENSE, International Conciliation pamphlet 555, New York, Carnegie Endowment for International Peace, 1965.

Sibley, Mulford, THE QUIET BATTLE, Doubleday-Anchor, New York, 1963. Anthology includes several selections bearing directly on this study.

Weinberg, Arthur and Lila (eds.), INSTEAD OF VIOLENCE, Grossman Publishers, New York, 1965.

Appendix

Members of Working Party of IN PLACE OF WAR:

An Inquiry into Nonviolent National Defense

WILLIAM DAVIDON. SSRS President, 1965-   ; Chairman Department of Physics at Haverford College, 1961-63, 1965-66; Fullbright Research Scholar, 1966-67.

JOHN M. SWOMLEY, JR. Professor of Christian Ethics at St. Paul School of Theology, Kansas City, Missouri; Executive Secretary of the Fellowship of Reconciliation, 1953-1960; Editor of *Current Issues;* author of the *The Military Establishment, America, Russia and the Bomb, The Road to War, The Peace Offensive and the Cold War, Press Agents of the Pentagon.*

A. J. MUSTE. (Deceased) National Chairman of the Committee for Nonviolent Action, one of the Editors of *Liberation* magazine; Executive Secretary of the Felllowship of Reconciliation, 1940-

63; Secretary Emeritus 1963; author of *Nonviolence in an Aggressive World, Not by Might;* Chairman of CNVA mission to Saigon, April 1966; Chairman of New York Fifth Avenue Peace Vietnam Parade Committee; Leader of mission to Hanoi, December 1966-January 1967.

MULFORD SIBLEY. Professor of Political Science at the University of Minnesota; visiting Professor of Political Science, Stanford University, 1957-58; visiting Professor of Government, Cornell University, 1962-63; contributed articles to the *American Political Science Review, Journal of Politics, American Quarterly, Hastings Law Journal;* author of *The Quiet Battle, Unilateral Initiatives and Disarmament.*

GEORGE LAKEY. Instructor at the Upland Institute of the Crozer Foundation; formerly Executive Secretary of Friends Peace Committee, Philadelphia Yearly Meeting of Friends; co-author of *A Manual for Direct Action;* author of *Nonviolent Action: How it Works;* participated in Civilian Defense Study Conference, Oxford, 1964.

CHARLES WALKER. College Program Director, AFSC, MAR; formerly Middle Atlantic Secretary of the Fellowship of Reconciliation; one of the founding editors of *Liberation* magazine; originator and co-chairman, Vigil at Fort Detrick; travelled in India and Far East 1963 to study training program for nonviolent action in India and participate in the Delhi-Peking Friendship March; author of *Organizing for Nonviolent Direct Action;* contributed to volume *Gandhi: His Relevance for our Times.*

JAMES E. BRISTOL. On staff of American Friends Service Committee 1947- ; AFSC representative in Zambia 1965- ; formerly director of AFSC Program on Nonviolence; pastor of Grace Lutheran Church, Camden, N.J. 1935-43; imprisoned 1941-1943 as conscientious objector to World War II; co-author of *Speak Truth To Power,* also author of pamphlets and magazine articles.

STEPHEN G. GARY. Associate Executive Secretary of American Friends Service Committee 1959- ; on AFSC staff 1946- ;

co-author of several AFSC published reports on foreign policy issues, including *The United States and the Soviet Union, Steps to Peace—A Quaker View of Foreign Policy, Speak Truth to Power.*

SIDNEY LENS. Author, lecturer, world traveler, trade union leader. Author of *Left, Right and Center, The Counterfeit Revolution, A World in Revolution, The Crisis of American Labor, Working Men, Africa-Awakening Giant, The Futile Crusade: Anti-Communism as American Credo,* contributed articles to numerous journals in the United States and abroad on labor and foreign policy. Travelled in eighty-one countries and lectured widely at universities and from public platforms.

STEWART MEACHAM. Secretary for Peace Education, American Friends Service Committee, 1959-   ; formerly Presbyterian pastor, regional director for National Labor Relations Board, Labor advisor in Korea, and director of Sidney Hillman Foundation. Co-author of *A New China Policy.*